CHICHESTER COLLEGE
WITHDRAWN
FROM LIBRARY STOCK

C267961

The Harrow XI 1869.

Manly & Muscular Diversions

*Public Schools and the Nineteenth-Century
Sporting Revival*

Tony Money
Archivist, Radley College

Duckworth

First paperback edition 2001
First published in 1997 by
Gerald Duckworth & Co. Ltd.
61 Frith Street, London W1D 3JL
Tel: 020 7434 4242
Fax: 020 7434 4420
Email: inquiries@duckworth-publishers.co.uk
www.ducknet.co.uk

© 1997 by Tony Money

All rights reserved. No part of this publication
may be reproduced, stored in a retrieval system, or
transmitted, in any form or by any means, electronic,
mechanical, photocopying, recording or otherwise,
without the prior permission of the publisher.

A catalogue record for this book is available
from the British Library

ISBN 0 7156 3152 7

CHICHESTER COLLEGE	
CHICHESTER CAMPUS	
Class.	Acc.No.
796.0941	C267961
ISBN	0 7156 3152 7

Typeset by Ray Davies
Printed and bound in Great Britain by
The Bath Press, Avon

Contents

To all colleagues, past and present, who on pitch, court, river and elsewhere have devoted so much time, energy and enthusiasm in the service of physical education and good sportsmanship.

Acknowledgements
& thanks to

The staff of the Bodleian Library, Oxford, the British Library, Bloomsbury and its Newspaper Library at Colindale.

My particular thanks go to School Archivists at Charterhouse, Clifton, Uppingham, Rugby, Shrewsbury and Westminster for the loan of illustrations, and to Peter Lawrence of Eton for the gift of the stereoscopic pictures.

I should also like to thank the undermentioned Archivists, Librarians, Headmasters, Headmasters' Secretaries and others for their kind help with information, all of which was of positive value in filling out the overall picture (even though sometimes the information received was negative): Peter Lawrence and Michael Meredith (Eton College); John Field, Valerie Johnston, David Chaundler, Peter Holmes and Jane Bland (Westminster School); John Leaf, John Ingram and A.D.K. Hawkyard (Harrow School); James Lawson (Shrewsbury School); John Marshall, Rusty MacLean and Jennifer Macrory (Rugby School); Mrs B. Freake, Ann Wheeler and Shirley Corke (Charterhouse); Simon Eliot and Steven Bailey (Winchester College); David West and Terry Rogers (Marlborough College); Richard Bland (Clifton College); the late Bryan Matthews, and Jerry Rudman (Uppingham School); David Kemp and Jean Cook (Tonbridge School); John Bowes (Cheltenham College); Revd Alan White (Bromsgrove School); John G. Davis (Leeds Grammar School); Frank Miles (King's College School); Alastair Macpherson and Mrs M. Bass (Haileybury); Paul Pollak (The King's School, Canterbury); Roderick Thomson, David Veall and Donald Haigh (Bradford Grammar School); Brian Martin (Magdalen College School); Janet Pennington (Lancing College); Michael Lewis (King Edward VII School, Sheffield); Michael Thornely (Sedbergh School); Tony Tinkel (The Oratory School); Janet Eason (City of London School); Gerald Wright (Forest School); Revd F.J.Turner (Stonyhurst College); Bill Surtees (Durham School); Warwick H. Brookes (Giggleswick School); John Dunlop (Merchiston Castle School); the late Michael Cherniavsky (Christ's Hospital); John F.M.Walker (Repton School); Mrs M.I. Cotton (Pocklington School); Peter King (Hurstpierpoint College); Revd T. Richardson (Ampleforth College); John V. Mitchell (St Peter's School, York); Revd Richard Jones (Douai School); Brian Nolan (King's School, Rochester); Alan Mitchell (Bolton School); Brian

Mains (Royal Grammar School, Newcastle upon Tyne); Paul Cattermole (Norwich School); L. Earnshaw (King William's College, Isle of Man); R.J. Brandon (Wolverhampton Grammar School); Dr D.T. Witcombe (Nottingham High School); A.H. Barfield (George Watson's College); C.W. Turner (The Glasgow Academy); B.J. Wilson and Godfrey Stott (Chigwell School); Miss G.M. Bakewell (Merchant Taylors' School, Northwood); John Warmington (Sherborne School); Felicity Given (Glenalmond College); Richard G. Miller (Bedford School); Nicholas Henshall (Stockport Grammar School); Commander R.H. Grist (Liverpool College); Keith Berry (The Perse School); John L. Barber (Oakham School); Jack Waddell (Aldenham School); F. Rogers (King Edward's School, Birmingham); Rodney Sturgeon (Kingston Grammar School); Neil Lyon (Wellingborough School); Michael Booker (Bristol Grammar School); John Duddell (Portsmouth Grammar School); Theodore Mallinson (Highgate School); David Warnes (Ipswich School); G.F. Dunkin (The Hulme Grammar School, Oldham); Michael Willis (Brentwood School); H.H.S. Spry-Leverton (Berkhamsted School); Ian Bailey (The Manchester Grammar School); Mick Dean, David Bland and Peter Way (Radley College); The Archivist (Blundell's School).

Patricia Coleman and Sylvia Pybus (Sheffield City Libraries); Kathryn McCord (Kensington Central Library); Derek English (Durham County Library); David M.N. Tinch (The Orkney Library); Chris Heane (Alnwick Area Public Library); P.W. Edgell (Alnwick Shrovetide Committee); Miss R. Brown (Borders Regional Library, Selkirk); Kathleen Mayo (Atherstone Library, Warwickshire); Pearl Webster (Ashbourne Library, Derbyshire).

Tim Chandler (Stanford University, California); Kevin Whelan (Royal Irish Academy); Danny Lynch (Cumann Luthchleas Gael); the late Richard Burnell; Tony Pocock (Kingswood Press); Robert Gieve (Gieves & Hawkes); the late Bill Liversidge (Abingdon); Christine Grindon (The Field); Brigadier A.D. Myrtle (The Tennis & Rackets Association); Paul Rossiter-Marvell (Blackheath Football Club); J.C. Rutherford (The Queen's Park Football Club); Jim Norris (Blackburn Rovers Football Club); Nottingham Forest Football Club; David Barber (The Football Association); Matthew Engel (Wisden's Cricketers' Almanack); Stephen Green (Lord's Cricket Ground); the late Dick Goodwin (Wirral).

Finally, special thanks to Leo Cooper for his very welcome encouragement, advice and enthusiasm and for his success in finding me a publisher; to Sue Brown for her endless, tireless reproduction of the first text and its many successors over the years; and to Jock Mullard for his expert, timely and extremely efficient transformation of the script and its accessories into a publisher-friendly package.

List of Illustrations

15. The Interior of a Jeu de Paume. (Bodleian Library, University of Oxford, 268 d 41 plate 12)
16. Scoring is similar to Lawn Tennis.
17. A tennis court at the Duke of Württemberg's New College at Tübingen, c. 1569. (Bodleian Library, University of Oxford, 268 d 41 plate 36)
18. 16th century Pallone in Italy. (Mary Evans Picture Library)
19a,b From Antonio Scaino (1555), *Trattato del giuoco della Palla.* (Bodleian Library, University of Oxford, Douce S 600 pp. 156-7, 158-9)
20. The future James VII and II. (Bodleian Library, University of Oxford, 268 d 41 plate 16)
21. The Five Chimneys, Tothill Fields. Now Vincent Square. (Westminster School Archives)
22. French Cricket (Bodleian Library, University of Oxford, 384 e 19 p. 300)
23. Cricket at the artillery ground in 1743, by B. Cole. (Hulton Getty)
24. New Articles of the Game of Cricket,1785. (Hulton Getty)
25. Merchant Taylors' School. (Mary Evans Picture Library)
26. View of Harrow, 1802. (Hulton Getty)
27. Lord's third cricket ground, before the fire destroyed the original pavilion in 1825. (Hulton Getty)
28. A game of single wicket cricket at Rugby School at the time of Dr Arnold's appointment in 1828. (Hulton Getty)
29. The Royal Shrewsbury School Hunt, by Sir Henry Dryden, 1834. (Shrewsbury School Archives).
30. The Huntsman, by Sir Henry Dryden, 1834. (Shrewsbury School Archives)
31. A 'Hot' at Foot Ball, Winchester. Twenty-two and Twenty-two in the 1830s. (Bodleian Library, University of Oxford, G.A. Hants 8° 73 frontispiece)
32. Charterhouse, 1805. The Cloisters in the background.(Hulton Getty)
33. Radley, 1859. Cricket in 'College caps'. (Radley College Archives)
34. Bradfield, 1865(Mary Evans Picture Library)
35 A Winchester Fives Court.
36. Little Dean's Yard, Westminster. (Westminster School Archives)
37. Shrewsbury, The Old School 1811. (Shrewsbury School Archives)
38. Hand Fives and Bat Fives, Marlborough, 1849, by G.F.Glennie in A.G. Bradley, A.C. Champneys & J.W. Baines (1923), *A History of Marlborough College*. (Bodleian Library, University of Oxford, G.A. Wiltshire 8° 91 p. 285)
39. Radley Fives Bats, by Rolfe Hayden. (Radley College Archives)
40. Radley in the 1890s. (Radley College Archives)
41. Eton Fives. (Hulton Getty)
42. Chapel steps, Eton. (Bodleian Library, University of Oxford, 38455 e 1 p. 415)

Chapter 1

Early Games

For centuries medieval upper class culture was military. Where a vassal owed military service to his feudal overlord, and ultimately to the king, his athletic exercise reflected images of battle accentuating this relationship. The Tournament was, hence, the great sport of the middle ages. It probably originated in France in the 11th century when, to display their skill and courage, bodies of armed horsemen fought mock battles, or *mêlées*. As weapons were blunted, death by impalement was rare: other causes prevailed. In 1240 at Neuss, near Cologne, for example, sixty knights died, mostly from suffocation. Despite papal interdicts and royal fears of gatherings of armed knights, the *mêlées* remained popular for a long time. The thrill of danger was an essential part of chivalry, and for the knights fighting was a passion.

In later centuries the *mêlée* was increasingly replaced by the joust, a mock duel on either side of the tilt, a wooden barrier. By charging 'at full tilt' the rider's aim was to unhorse his opponent or break his own blunted, narrow-shafted lance by a well-timed strike on shield or helm. Knights and squires practised jousting, and pages learnt it on the quintain, a revolving wooden figure fitted with a shield and a bar, weighted with sandbag or club that swung round and knocked a slow tilter off his horse.

Jousting was reserved for those of noble birth. In France, the home of chivalry, the knights held it unchivalrous to kill a man at a distance; a folly that cost them dear at Crécy, Poitiers and Agincourt. The long bow with accurate range of up to 300 yards was the most successful weapon of the English in the Hundred Years War. For the common people archery was both a necessary duty and a sport, to be learnt from an early age and regularly practised on Sundays and feast days at the parish butts. To encourage constant practice of the bow, prizes for archery were often offered at village fêtes and pageants. Other common sports were running, jumping, throwing the stone, and wrestling, exercises to strengthen the sinews; and hunting, which not only provided exercise and excitement, but also food for the pot. There were other, less useful games, which distracted the common people from their practice at the butts, and which thus incurred royal displeasure. Among these were (foot)ball games which attracted large numbers of players.

Early Football in England and Scotland

The first possible mention of football in England is in William Fitzstephen's 'Descriptio Nobilissimae Civitatis Londoniae' in 1174, written as a preface to his *Life of Thomas à Becket*.

> Every year on the day which is called the Carnival [Shrove Tuesday], ... to begin with the boys' games (for we were all boys once), all the boys in each school bring their master their game-cocks, and the whole morning is devoted to the boys' play, they having a holiday to look on at the cock-fights in their school. After the mid-day meal the entire youth of the city goes into the fields for the famous game of ball. [*Post prandium, exit in campos omnis iuventus urbis ad lusum pilae celebrem.*] The scholars of each school have their ball; and nearly all the holders of civic office also provide one. The older people, the fathers, and the rich men of the city come on horseback to see the contests of the young, and in their fashion sport with the young men; and there seems to be aroused in them a stirring of natural heat, by watching so much activity and by sharing in the delight of the freedom of youth.

The first unequivocal mention of football occurs much later in 1314 (when Edward II was on his way to defeat at Bannockburn), made in a Proclamation for the Preservation of the Peace by the Lord Mayor of London:

> Whereas our Lord the King is going towards the parts of Scotland, in his war against his enemies, and has especially commanded us strictly to keep his peace ... And whereas there is great uproar in the City, through certain tumults arising from great footballs in the fields of the public [*Et pur ceo qe graunt noise est en la Cite, par ascunes rageries de grosses pelotes de pee ferir en prees du poeple*], from which many evils perchance may arise – which God forbid – we do command and do forbid, on the King's behalf, upon pain of imprisonment, that such game shall be practised henceforth within the City ...

The popularity of football games had grown considerably since 1174 and there was a practical purpose behind Edward III's order of 1365:

> To the sheriffs of London. Order to cause proclamation to be made that every able-bodied man of the said city on feast-days when he has leisure shall in his sports use bows and arrows or pellets or bolts ... forbidding them under pain of imprisonment to meddle in the hurling of stones, loggats and quoits, handball, football [*pilam pedivam*] ... or other vain games of no value; as the people of the realm, noble and simple, used heretofore to practise the said art in their sports, whence by God's help came forth honour to the kingdom and advantage to the King in his actions of war. *And now the said art is almost wholly disused, and the people indulge in the games aforesaid and in other dishonest and unthrifty or idle games whereby the realm is like to be without archers.*

The victory of Crécy in 1346 had shown the importance of the long bow. But that the successive bans on football were disregarded is shown by the interdict of Richard II in 1388:

> ... but such Servants and Labourers shall have Bows and Arrows, and use the same on Sundays and Holydays, and leave all playing at ball, whether handball or football (*à la main comme à piée*) ... and other such importune games ...

Henry V in 1414, the year before Agincourt, outlawed football and other games and ordered the practice of the bow. His crushing victory increased the fame of the English and Welsh longbow men, who had no equal in Europe, and gave added weight to the ban. But to little avail. In 1477 Edward IV issued an edict:

> Item. That according to the laws of this land no person shall practise any unlawful games such as dice, quoits, football, and such games, but that every strong and able-bodied person shall practise with his bow for the reason that the national defence depends much on bowmen. [*mez que chascune persone potent et able en corps useroit son arke par cause que la defence de cest terre estoise meult par archers.*]

Under Henry VII and Henry VIII numerous statutes were passed against unlawful games. Even under Henry VIII and Queen Elizabeth landowners could be punished for allowing football to be played on their land. One reason is that England persisted with archers longer than any other European state. Henry VIII laid down strict and exact conditions which emphasise the continuing importance of the long bow.

> Every of the kynges subjectes nat lame decrepite nor maymed ... within the age of lx yeres ... excepte spirituall men ... shall use and exercyse shotynge in long Bowes, and have a bowe and arowes redy contynually in his house to use shotynge, Bill for the Maintaining of Artillery and the Debarring of Unlawful Games, 1541.

He was also responsible for providing a bow and two arrows for any boy in his house between the ages of 7 and 17 and for training him in shooting. If the boy was a servant, the master was to deduct the cost of bow and arrows from his wages. Failure to provide the equipment led to an automatic fine of 6 shillings and 8 pence a month. But circumstances changed slowly, and the Privy Council in 1595 ordered that archers should no longer be enrolled in the trained bands, but only arquebusiers, caliver-men and musketeers. Probably the last time that archers were in action in Europe was on the Ile de Ré in Buckingham's Siege of La Rochelle in 1627. (The Act, however, remained on the statute book for three centuries until its repeal in 1845.)

In Scotland football was as popular as it was in England, judging by successive royal bans.

James I 1424	Item. It is statut and the King forbiddes that no man play at the futball under payne of ivd to be paid to the lord of the land as often as he be taynted [convicted], or to the sheriff of the land or to his agents, if the lords are unwilling to punish such trespasses.
James II 1457	... futball and golfe be utterly cryed down and not to be used.
James IV 1491	... in no place in this realm that be used futeball, golfe, or other sik unprofitable sports.

But from the accounts of the Lord High Treasurer for Scotland in 1497

> Item: The 22nd day of April, given to James Dog to buy footballs for the King ... 2s.

James VI's *Basilikon Doron, His Majesty's Instructions to his Dearest Sonne, Henry the Prince* was privately printed in 1599 and published in Edinburgh in 1603, in which year he succeeded Queen Elizabeth as King James I of England. In it he wrote

> From this Coast I debar all rough and violent exercises, as the football, meeter for laming, than making able the users thereof.

In England in the 16th century King James's opinion of football as a rough and violent exercise was anticipated by Sir Thomas Elyot in *The Booke Named the Governour* (1531)

> ... foote balle, wherein is nothing but beastly furie and extreme violence; wherof procedeth hurte and consequently rancour and malice do remaine with them that be wounded; wherefore it is to be put in perpetuall silence.

In 1583 the Puritan pampleteer Philip Stubbes in *The Anatomy of Abuses in the Realm of England* gives an account of football as he saw it:

> Any exercise which withdraweth us from godlines, either upon the Sabaoth or any other day els is wicked and to be forbiden ... For as concerning football playing ... it may rather be called a friendly kind of fight then a play or recreation, a bloody and murthering practise then a felowly sporte or pastime. For dooth not everyone lye in weight for his adversarie, seeking to overthrow him and to picke [pitch] him on his nose, though it be upon hard stones? In ditch or dale, in valley or hil, or what place soever it be, hee careth not so he have him down ... so that by this meanes, sometimes their necks are broken, sometimes their arms ... for they have the sleights to meet one betwixt two, to

1. 'I would now make a safe retreat, but that methinks I am stopped by one of your heroic games called foot-ball; which I conceive (under your favour) not very conveniently civil in the streets'. Sir William Davenant's description of London in 1634, quoted in William Hone's (1827), *Table Book*.

dash him against the hart with their elbowes, to hit him under the short ribbes with their griped fists, and with their knees to catch him upon the hip and to pick him on his neck, with a hundered such murdering devices: and hereof groweth envie, malice, rancour, cholor, hatred, displeasure, enmitie, and what not els: and sometimes fighting, brawling, contention, quarrel picking, murther, homicide, and great effusion of blood, as experience dayly teacheth.

Football in England was often a hard and brutal game, as the above descriptions plainly show, and as numerous reports of death from it confirm. This was reason enough for clerical censure to join royal displeasure. But football persisted in the 17th century, despite the Puritans and prosecutions for playing or watching football on Sunday. It was played under the Commonwealth, perhaps because Oliver Cromwell had been a footballer himself. According to a Royalist pamphleteer (in 1663) after the Restoration, while at Sidney Sussex College, Cambridge, 'he was more famous for his exercises in the Feilds than in the Schools, in which he never had the honour of, because no worth and merit to a degree, being one of the chief Match makers and Players at Foot-ball, Cudgels or any other boystrous sport or game'.

*

In 16th-century England there was one lone voice raised in favour of football. Two years before Philip Stubbes' diatribe in *The Anatomy of Abuses*, Richard Mulcaster (1532-1611) published in 1581 his '*Positions wherein those primitive circumstances be examined, which are necessary for the training up of children, either for skill in their booke, or health in their bodie*'. It was written in English, not Latin, and was addressed to Queen Elizabeth. Mulcaster, who had been educated at Eton, was the first Master of Merchant Taylors' School founded by the Company in 1561 in St Laurence Pountneie. He had advanced views, favouring the education of girls, and believing that one teacher should be responsible for both the physical and the intellectual welfare of a pupil. He quarrelled with the Company because he had increased his meagre remuneration by taking boys beyond the statutory number. He was censured and directed to dismiss the supernumerary boys. He resigned with the Parthian shot *Fidelis servus, perpetuus asinus*. He later became High Master of St Paul's. In *Positions*, in the chapter 'Of the Ball' he writes of football:

> ... the Football play, which could not possibly have growne to this greatness, that it is now at, nor have been so much used, as it is in all places, if it had not had great helpes, both to health and strength, and to me the abuse of it is a sufficient argument, that it hath a right use: which being revoked to his primative *will both helpe, strength, and comfort nature*: though as it is now commonly used, with thronging of a rude multitude, with bursting of shinnes, and breaking of legges, it be neither civil, neither worthy the name of any traine to health. Wherein any man may evidently see the use of the trayning maister. For if one stand by, which can judge of the play, and is judge of the parties, and hath authority to commande in the place, all those inconveniences have been, I know, and will be I am sure very lightly redressed, nay they will never entermedle in the matter, neither shall there be complaint, where there is no cause. Some smaller number with such overlooking, sorted into sides and standings, not meeting with their bodies so boisterously to trie their strength: not shouldring or shuffing one another so barbarously, and using to walke after, may use football for as much good to the body, by the chief use of legges, as the Armeball [Italian Pallone], for the same, by the use of the armes. And being so used, the Footeball strengtheneth and brawneth the whole body, and by provoking superfluities downeward, it dischargeth the head, and upper partes, it is good for the bowells, and to drive down the stone and gravell from both the bladder and kidneies. It helpeth weak hammes, by much moving, beginning at a meane, and simple shankes by thickening of the flesh, no less than riding doth. Yet rash running and to much force oftentimes breaketh some inward conduit, and bringeth ruptures.

Mulcaster for his book made extensive use of the *De arte gymnastica*, by the Italian professor of medicine and editor of Hippocrates, Girolamo Mercuriali (Hieronymus Mercurialis 1530-1603), first published in Venice in 1569 and in Paris in 1577. He finishes with 'The most of these notes, which I have alleaged, were given in Italie, Greece & Spaine, and that climate farre distant, and much differing from our degree.' Indeed football in Italy was very different socially from the game in England.

Football in Italy

In England football was played by apprentices and artisans in the towns, and in the country by peasantry and yeomanry. In Italy football, in the form of Calcio, was a game for gentlemen and noblemen.

The first sure mention of Calcio is at the beginning of the 15th century in an anonymous poem describing a game in the Piazza Santo Spirito, Florence. In 1490 and 1491 games were played on the frozen Arno, between the Ponte Vecchio and Ponte Santa Trinità. Matches took place on the Prato, the open area along the river used for parades and exercises of the Florentine army. But for the sumptuous Calcio in Livrea the venue was one of the Piazzas – Santo Spirito, Santa Maria Novella or Santa Croce.

Although Calcio at Florence was the most famous, forms of it were played in other northern cities, Padua, Venice, Pisa, Mondovi (Piedmont), and elsewhere. The first book on the game was written by a student of Padua University, at that time Europe's leading university: *Treatise on the Game of Ball* by Antonio Scaino da Salò, published in Venice in 1555. The seventy-second and final chapter describes how Calcio was played at Padua:

This game is played with a ball full of wind, weighing 11 ounces, and 7 inches in diameter ... in an area longer than a stone's throw by however strong an arm, and scarcely half as wide; and if it is surrounded by a wall on every side it is very convenient ... A player can hit the ball with any part of his body, when it is in the air and after it bounces, and he can kick it with his feet while it is rolling on the ground, pick it up, hold it in his hand, and carry it (a glorious feat) into the enemy goal. He is only forbidden, with the ball in his hand, to throw it; and when this happens it results in a scrum [*scaramuccia* = skirmish, scrimmage] ...

The ground is divided into two equal parts and the ball is placed in the middle. The two sides are distinguished by their dress. The sign being given by a drum or a trumpet, one of the players ... gives the ball a kick, at which, of course, immediately a scrimmage is formed, so that everyone is permitted to pick up the ball, hit it and pursue it towards the opposition goal. From this method of starting the game with a kick of the foot, it was, perhaps, named the game of *Calcio* [kick].

Every team has to have a captain, who will choose suitable players, some of whom are good runners, others strong at holding up the opposition attack, others good at stopping the ball, and some who are skilled at forming a scrimmage, and these will stand in the front of the battle as vanguard. Behind these will be placed the strong players, and behind them the runners. The rearguard will have those who are skilled and experienced at stopping the ball ...

The players placed in front, if they do not have a good opportunity to strike a blow, should leave the ball to those who are behind them, meanwhile confronting their opponents to prevent them getting downfield. The runner who has to run down the field with the ball in his hand will have the support of some of the strong men, and the vanguard will confront their adversaries in order to give him a quick and free passage. That runner, having space and opportunity, will run right into the enemy goal-area, but seeing himself attacked by too many opponents, he will check his run and without losing a moment of time will strike the ball, and rather with a kick than otherwise, because such a shot is safer as it is less easy to stop ...

The game at Florence was much more of a spectacle, conducted with great ceremony. In 1580, twenty-five years after Scaino's book was published in Venice, Count Giovanni de' Bardi, Director of Calcio in Florence, published his *Discourse on the Game of Calcio*.

... This game being extremely hard work, it cannot comfortably last beyond the cold season. It stretches from the beginning of January to the end of March. But because Calcio is a spectacle, where the bigger the number of spectators, the more attractive it is, the days of the

2. The site of the old Roman Amphitheatre at Padua, destroyed by Attila's horde in 455. A game of Calcio 1596. 'I do not think it is possible to find a ground more suitable for it than the Arena of Padua, where the scholars at the time of Lent, in very great numbers are accustomed to practise this battle, with 20, 30 or 40 a side ... At each end, according to the length of the railing, a space is marked off into which those who want to win have to place the ball.' Antonio Scaino da Salò (1555) *Treatise on the Game of Ball*

Festival of Bacchus, that is Carnival, are dedicated to the more ceremonial games of Calcio.

The most celebrated game of Calcio was played on 17 February 1530, in the last years of the Republic. The city had been under siege for three months by 40,000 Spanish, German and Italian troops of the army of the Emperor Charles V.

> The young men in order not to interrupt the ancient custom of playing Calcio each year at Carnival time, and also to show their contempt for the enemy, had a game in livery in the Piazza Santa Croce, 25 Whites and 25 Greens [representing different quarters of the city], playing for the prize of a calf; and to be not only heard but seen, they sent a part of the band with trumpets and other instruments on to the ridge of the roof of Santa Croce, where from the hill of Giramonte a cannonball was fired at them; but the shot went high and did no harm to anyone.[1]

After the fall of the Republic and the installation of the Medici Dukes of Florence, the principal games were played not just at Carnival, but on important political occasions also.

> The game of Calcio, for which the Florentines nurse an unconfined passion, assumed particular solemnity on the occasion of princely weddings and illustrious visits.[2]

The first Duke, Alessandro, caused a Calcio to be played in 1532 when he presented the ring to his 12-year-old betrothed, Margherita of Austria, bastard of Charles V. In 1558, for the festivities at the wedding of a daughter of Cosimo I to the eldest son of the Duke of Ferrara, there were two Calcios in Livery.

> The best players among the young men made up two teams, one dressed in yellow satin, the other in white satin, and eight officials in brocade of the same colour, and their banner in the same colours, and they also had a pavilion above the piazza and one below so that they could rest there and refresh with confections and *trebbiano* [white wine] the trumpeters, drummers and ball-bearers.[2]

Those not chosen to play determined to have their own game a few days later in a different piazza.

> Because they knew they were not such good players as those of Santa Croce, they wanted at least to defeat them in their dress; one side was dressed in silver brocade and the other in gold brocade, and the banners were made and the ball-bearers, trumpeters and drummers were suited, and the piazza of Santa Maria Novella was levelled and squared off ... and knowing that the Duke Cosimo de' Medici and don Francesco, Prince of Florence, and the Prince of Ferrara and all the Court were in attendance,the players appeared so superbly dressed that they earned the admiration of all the spectators. It was a rich but not a vigorous Calcio, because they were bad defenders, bad forwards, and not very good midfielders.[2]

3. The Piazza Santa Croce at Florence. A Calcio in Livery about to begin 1580. The playing area is surrounded by a wooden fence roughly 100 x 50 metres and 1 metre high. A team consists of 27 players: 15 *corridori / innanzi* (runners / forwards) divided into three groups of 5 on left, centre and right; 5 *sconciatori* (strong pushers) lining up in midfield; in defence 3 *datori* as full-backs and 4 as goalkeepers. The goal, unlike that of Padua was the whole of the 50 metres end-fence – so 4 goalkeepers were needed. A goal was scored when the ball was struck either by a closed fist or by a kick, full pitch over the fence.

Calcio could not be played by everyone, 'no artisans or servants, but honoured Soldiers, Gentlemen, Lords and Princes. Those chosen to play Calcio will be Gentlemen from 18 to 45 years, or more or less according to temperament, of good repute, well regarded, and agreeable.' During the season teams were chosen from those who turned up for the evening game. For the game in Livery teams were announced two days beforehand.

Half of the 34 rules of the game, published in 1673, are concerned with the pre-match ceremonial. The parade was led by trumpeters, then drummers, then the *Innanzi* (forwards) in pairs one red, one blue (say), followed by a blue and a red, and so on. Then follow the Standard bearers preceded by more drummers. Then the *Sconciatori* (midfielders), and the *Datori* (defenders) the senior of whom carry balls. Being filled with air, they were liable to be deflated. 'Having paraded once round the piazza, they turn towards that part where the most important spectators are seated, and the standards are handed over to soldiers of the Guard of his Serenity the Grand Duke to hold in front of the Pavilion at either end.'[3] At the first sound of the Trumpet the retinue retires from the field; at the second the players take up their positions; at the third the Ball-Bearer, dressed in both colours, from the side of the ground hits the ball to start the game. If this whole ritual was not carried out properly, it would have to be done all over again.

The last game of Calcio in Livery at Florence was played in Piazza Santa Croce in 1739 in front of Francis II, Duke of Lorraine, who had succeeded the Medicis as Grand Duke, and his wife Maria Teresa, Empress of Austria. After this break with the past, and also because the piazzas were by now filled with statues, benches and trees, the game fell into disuse.

In 1930, at the quatercentenary of the siege of Florence, the game was revived and it is now played annually in the Piazza Signoria which is covered with a thick layer of sand, with great pageantry, in front of considerable numbers of Florentines and tourists.

It is difficult to imagine any connection or mutual influence between the football played by the common people all over England and

DISCORSO

SUL CALCIO
FIORENTINO
D'ONDE SI HA L'ORIGINE DEL CALCIO IN GENERALE

S' AGGIUNGONO IN QUEST' IMPRESSIONE

I CAPITOLI E PIANTA DEL CALCIO DI LIVORNO DEL PRESENTE ANNO 1766.

DATO DALL' INCLITA NAZIONE INGLESE

PER LA VENUTA DI S. A. R. SERENISSIMA

PIETRO LEOPOLDO
PRINCIPE REALE D' UNGHERIA E DI BOEMIA, ARCIDUCA D' AUSTRIA E GRANDUCA DI TOSCANA,

E S. A. R. SERENISSIMA

MARIA LUISA
INFANTA DI SPAGNA, ARCIDUCHESSA D' AUSTRIA GRANDUCHESSA DI TOSCANA.

LIVORNO

****

Per MARCO COLTELLINI)(Con *Approvazione*.

4. 'The Calcio of Livorno presented by the Illustrious English Nation for the visit of their Serene Highnesses the Archduke and Archduchess of Austria, Grandduke and Grandduchess of Tuscany in the year 1766.' John (Giovanni) Dick, the British Consul at Leghorn (Livorno), put on two games of Calcio for the occasion. The last game in Florence had been played in 1739. The main difference from the old rules of Florence was that matches were 50 a side. A number of English names appear on the team lists, and several weeks were spent in practising the game. The first match betwen the Reds and the Blues took place on 20th May. 'The game would have been magnificent beyond measure, had not great disputes arisen between the two teams. The time that they spent in long arguments every time they went for the ball really annoyed the spectators. Playing time was less than a quarter of an hour, interrupted by disputes and the time taken by the comings and goings of the judges.' The second match was more successful and was won by the Blues.

the aristocratic games of Calcio played in the northern cities of Italy, with their written rules, their colourful ceremonies, their restricted season and playing area, and their ducal patronage. Unfortunately there are no written rules or descriptions of football games played in Britain until the Shrove Tuesday games, which came relatively late. It is quite possible that there were games of football which resembled Calcio. The word football obviously suggests more use of the feet, but hands are used in all forms of football played today.

Football in France

If there was foreign influence on early English football, it came from France. An early reference to football (La Soule) in France occurs in an edict of Philip V (the Tall) in 1319:

> We forbid the playing of dice, quoits, skittles, soules and similar games, by which our subjects are in no way practised in the use of arms for defence of our realm, and we command that they learn to practise and apply themselves to the act of drawing the crossbow or the longbow in public places. [*discant se exercere et habilitare in facto tractus baliste vel arcus in locis publicis*].

The *soule* (*solle*) or *choule* (*cholle*) was a ball which was made sometimes of wood, sometimes of leather, according to the region; in the latter case it was filled with moss, bran, animal hair, sawdust or similar stuffing, or it was blown up with air. It was propelled by foot or by hand or by a curved stick, and was played mostly in the countryside over large tracts of land or along stretches of the public highway. The game was found in various places throughout France, but latterly mainly to the north of the Loire, in Brittany, Normandy and Picardy in particular. The formal game was usually played between parishes or two parts of the same parish, the object being to bring the ball back to a fixed 'goal' within one's own parish or area.

La Soule was a 'feudal right according to which a vassal had to present the soule, once a year, to the seigneur of the place, who as president of the game had the privilege of throwing it to the people on days fixed by custom'.[4] In several areas this feudal right remained in force until the Revolution. Generally it was the man last married who had the duty of offering the *soule* to the seigneur. In this way the seigneur had control over the game and could limit it to one day a year, if he so wished.

> I am convinced that the monopoly of the droit de soule given to the seigneurs was simply a policing measure ... the seigneurs only allowed one day in the year and to certain people.[5]

> At Vitré in Brittany delivery of the soule was made on the name day of Saint Stephen in a little chapel dedicated to the saint, and at the most solemn moment of the Mass, between the two elevations of the host.[6]

5. La Soule in Brittany. When M. le Maire throws up *la soule*, all the players rush to seize it. He who is lucky enough to grab it is furiously attacked by his opponents, who try to relieve him of his precious trophy, and is defended vigorously by his own side ... At this moment the spectator sees a confused mass of people who seem intent on crushing each other. Those on the outside try to seize by force the place of those at the centre, who defend themselves tooth and nail. These ceaseless individual efforts impart to the mass a most curious motion; now it is directed to the right, now to the left; most often it turns slowly on itself. It resembles some fantastic animal with a thousand heads and a thousand feet. Alexander Sorel (1894), *Le Jeu de la Choule*

The usual days for playing varied from place to place. The most common day was Shrove Tuesday (*mardi gras*) before the rigours of Lent. Elsewhere it was *mi-carême* (half-Lent) or Easter Monday, and according to one authority the clergy '*choulaient*' on Easter Day in the cloisters of churches and cathedrals or in the church itself.[7]

Apart from these fixed days the game was played mostly in winter on Sundays or Saints day holidays, and it was against these that royal wrath was directed. Fifty years after the edict of Philippe le Long, Charles V issued:

> *Lettres royales portant defense de jouer à la choule – En nostre hotel de St pol-lez-Paris, 3 avril 1369, 5° du règne. CHARLES, par la grace de Dieu, roy de France, à tous ceux qui ces présentes lettres verront, salut. Savoir faisons que nous désirans de tout nostre cuer le bon estat, seurté et defense de nostre royaume, de la chose publique et de tous nos subgiez ...* have forbidden and do forbid by these presents all games of dice, of paume, of skittles, of quoits, of solles, of billard [de terre: a form of croquet] and of all other such games which have no part in training for the defence of our realm on penalty of forty Paris sous ... And we desire and ordain that our said subjects should choose their games and pastimes *à eulx exercer et habiliter en fait de trait d'arc ou d'arbaleste ès biaux lieux et places convenables à ce ...*

Numerous *lettres de rémission*, or pardons, issued in the 14th and 15th centuries show that La Soule was a dangerous game and also a popular one, despite the prohibitions against it. In 1357 when Charles was still the Dauphin, he was ruling the country in place of his father, King John, who the year before had been taken prisoner by Edward, the Black Prince, at Poitiers. In *lettres de rémission* written from Cergy-Pontoise near Paris he approved the pardon accorded by the Queen to several individuals who had injured others while they '*estoient allez esbattre a un geu appelé chole qu'on faisait ou terrouer de Tombes, ainsi comme on avait accoustume de faire chacun an*'. This pardon was given in accordance with the Queen's right, the first time she entered a town, to absolve and set free all prisoners held or detained for every kind of crime.

One form of La Soule was played with a curved stick, reinforced with iron in the form of a cross, from which came the expression to *jouer à la crosse* or *crosser*. This dangerous implement was the cause of many deaths, as the *lettres de rémission* show:

> *Lettres de rémission en faveur de Willardin Hamart Mars 1387.*
>
> *Willardin Hamart, povre varlet et misérable ... et plusieurs autres jéunes gens feussent aléz par un jour de dimanche en une certaine place de terre située entre la ville de Wime et la ville de Hannencourt en Vimeu* [in Picardy] *... pour esbatre à un certain jeu appellé chole de la crosse ... Willardin Hamart feust d'une des parties et un appellé Thassin la Fosse de l'autre et ...* by chance the ball of the said game was sent high in the air in front of him and Thassin. And when Willardin saw the said ball coming, trying to hit it so as to send it far away, he struck with his crosse and by accident ... the blow of Willardin's crosse fell on the forehead of Thassin, from which blow, three weeks afterwards, Thassin died.
>
> Pardon for Willardin who fearing the rigour of justice has disappeared and has been issued a summons by the provost of Vimeu.
>
> *Donné à Paris ou mois de mars, l'an de grace mil CCC IIII*[xx] *et sept et de notre règne le VIII°.*

6. The goal was often ... a stream, pond, the sea or other water.

La Soule was also played in towns, but not so much as football was regularly played in the streets of London. The Police Authority of Amiens issued an ordinance in 1464:

> To avoid the quarrels, the grudges, the altercations, the troubles that have been caused before this and could occur after them by cholles that by custom have been made each year on the eve and the day of mardi gras, henceforth cholles will not be played on the said days.

In the countryside the game was played by all classes. The manuscript diary of Gilles, Sire de Gouberville et du Mesnil-au-Val, in the 16th century, contains many references to La Soule, which show it to have been a very important activity in the life of a country gentleman. Gouberville and le Mesnil are in the Cotentin Peninsula of Normandy, east of Cherbourg. As possessor of *un nom de seigneurie*, Gilles had certain judicial functions in his lands. He lived in his manor house with an extended family of legitimate and illegitimate relations and fourteen servants. It was customary to start the game

7. La Crosse in Brittany 1835. In 1636 a French Jesuit missionary, in what is now Ontario, saw a game called baggataway played by the Huron tribe, similar to La Crosse, and he gave it the name. Played by very many tribes in Canada and the U.S.A. Adopted by Canadians as Lacrosse.

of La Soule near a rural chapel. The players heard Mass there before starting.

Friday 15 January 1551. St Maur's Day. We went all together to St Maur [Chapel] and were the rest of the day at choule, which lasted up to twilight. There were present le sieur de Couriac capitaine de Cherebourg, le sieur Mareschal, Pierre de Sainct Jehan and more than 500 other persons both from one side and the other. Cantepye had a fall backwards, Monsieur Guillaume Le Lièvre, on top of him arse on to groin through the fault of Jehan Roger of Cherbourg. Cantepye thought to die, and remained a long time near fainting. [Cantepye was betrothed to Gouberville's bastard half-sister.]

Sunday 17 January 1551. I do not budge from here. I was not at Vespers nor at the Mass because I was so tired from la choule of St Maur that I could not be present.

Monday 15 January 1552. Before I had risen Quineville, Groult and Ozouville, soldier from the fort, arrived here coming from Valognes. We had breakfast together, then went to St Maur, they, Cantepye, Symmonet, Moisson, Lajoye, Gaultier-Birette [relatives and servants] and several others. We arrived there as Mass was being said, after which maître Robert Potet ... threw the ball and it was contested until about an hour before sunset and brought as far as Bretteville where Gratian Cabart seized it and won. [This was 6 or 7 kilometres from St Maur's chapel.

Christmas Eve 1555. On the said day at la Soule inside le clos Berger, Cantepye pushed me so hard with his fist, in running against me, on the right breast that it made me lose my voice and with great difficulty could I be brought back here. I thought I would faint on the way and lost my sight for almost half an hour, because of which I had to take to my bed [for four days].

17 January 1556. After Vespers I started to chouller and fell on my knee so hard that I tore my breeches along with their lining from my knee as far as the middle of my thigh.

24 July 1556. The curé of Tourlaville left here in the morning (it was a Sunday) and went to say Mass at Tourlaville, then he came back at Vespers. He hit at choulle [*à la crosse*] all the rest of the day. He supped and slept here.

Brittany did not finally become part of France until 1547, so, in contrast to Normandy, the earlier edicts of the French kings had no power over the Bretons, whose game was particularly fierce and dangerous. However, other authorities could use more than temporal threats. Raoul, Bishop of Tréguier published this Synodal statute in 1490.

The law attests that dangerous and pernicious games must be prohibited, because of the hatreds, rancour and enmity which, under the cover of recreational enjoyment, accumulate in many hearts, and of which a fatal occasion reveals the venom. We have learned, through the reports of men worthy of trust, that in several parishes and other places subject to our jurisdiction, on holidays and on other days, now for a very long time, a certain very pernicious and dangerous game is played, with a round, large and powerful ball, a game that is called in the vulgar tongue *mellat*. [A local name = ball.] From it already many scandals have resulted, and it is manifest that more serious ones will come from it in the future, if no timely remedy is found. That is why we forbid this dangerous and scandalous game, and declare *liable to the punishment of excommunication* and of a fine of one hundred sous those in our diocese, of whatever rank or condition, who would have the audacity or the pretension to play the said game.[8]

In 1686 La Soule was forbidden by the *Parlement* of Brittany, though the ban was widely ignored. In the next century the local authority at Pont-l'Abbé banned La Soule after a very fiercely contested game, in the course of which some fifty players were drowned in the bay which washes the walls of the town in southern Brittany. Little by little the dangers of the game to life and limb and the bans imposed on it had their effect; but it was the Revolution that effectively finished it off. Even before it the feeling against the privileges and feudal rights of the seigneurs affected the game. In the *Observations sommaires sur quelque droits féodaux relativement à la Bretagne* by Le Guével, lawyer at Josselin in 1789, the first of the feudal rights called '*odieux*' is *le droit de soule*. In the same year the people of Rennes, in their list of grievances presented to the Estates-General, called for the abolition of La Soule.

The game did continue in its different forms, though in a very reduced way, particularly in the Morbihan in southern Brittany around Vannes, and in the Cotentin Peninsula of Normandy, until the 19th century, and in Picardy around Compiègne until the early 20th century.

The Celtic Fringe

As a result of successive invasions the Celtic people have been pushed to the extremes of their territory, but, despite the differences between the various games, there is enough similarity to hint at a common family origin. Games using a silver ball (to represent the sun?) are found in Cornwall, and of old, in Ireland, as well as in France, giving some credibility to the sun-worship theory. Their related languages survive, but under continuous threat from either French or English. Cornish and Manx are no longer spoken.

Brittany

In his *Antiquité de la nation et de la langue des Celtes, autrement appelés Gaulois*, published in Paris in 1703, Paul Pezron wrote:

> I will say in passing, à propos the word *soul*, that the Armorican Bretons have a certain game, or quite singular exercise, that they call La Soule. They throw into the air, with all their strength, a kind of *boule*, or black leather ball filled with hair or hay; and when it falls, they all together lift their hands to receive it, and make a thousand attempts to try to catch it and to carry it away by running. For with them it is an act of bravery, I speak of the peasants, to succeed in getting it. I have no doubt at all that this round ball, that they call *soule*, was *invented by the ancient Gauls in honour of the Sun*, called by them *soul*, and that is why they throw it up high. Nowadays it is no more than a simple bodily exercise, like running or wrestling.

Emile Souvestre, author of *Les Derniers Bretons* in 1854, agrees that the game was a last vestige of the Celts' worship of the sun. He claims the ball was almost always adorned in bright colours to resemble the sun.

> For the ball by its spherical shape represented the sun. It was thrown into the air, as if to make it touch the sun's rays, and when it fell back it was fought for as a sacred object. The name *soule* itself comes from the Celtic *héault* (sun), in which the initial letter H has been changed into S as in all foreign words adopted by the Romans, which has produced *séaul* or *soul*.

Each side fought to take the *soule* back to its own village, where the 'goal' was often a hole in the ground, or a stream, pond, the sea, or other water. Placing the ball in the hole could be interpreted as an attempt to capture the sun's heat for the young crops, thus providing a better harvest than that of the neighbouring village. Dipping the ball into water could represent the rain needed for the crops.

> After Christianity had become established in the Western world – 'to destroy not but rather bend the pagan customs and usages to the service of God' – the connection between sun and water was in a measure maintained, and rain could still, it was believed, be procured by dipping the Cross, or the relics of a saint, into a well and scattering the water adhering to them on the surrounding ground; such, for example, was a custom observed till within recent years at the Fontaine de Barenton ... near Ploërmel in Brittany. 'Football a Survival of Magic?' W. Branch Johnson in: *The Contemporary Review* (1929)

Cornwall

In The Survey of Cornwall by Richard Carew, published in 1723, there is the description of a game similar in some respects to La Soule:

> Hurling taketh his denomination from throwing of the ball,[9] and is of two sorts, in the East parts of Cornwall, to goales, and in West, to the countrey.
>
> For hurling to goales, there are 15, 20 or 30 players more or lesse, chosen out on each side, who strip themselves into their slightest apparell,and then joyne hands in ranke one against another. Out of these ranks they match themselves by payres, one embracing another, & so passe away: every of which couple are specially to watch one another during the play.
>
> After this, they pitch two bushes in the ground, some eight or ten foote asunder; and directly against them, ten or twelve score off, other twayne in like distance, which they terme their Goales ... There is assigned for their gard, a couple of their best stopping Hurlers: the residue draw into the midst between both goales, where some indifferent person throweth up a ball, the which whosoever can catch, and carry through his adversaries goale, hath wonne the game. But therein consisteth one of Hercules his labours: for hee that is once possessed of the ball, hath his contrary mate waiting at inches, and assaying to lay hold upon him. The other thrusteth him in the brest, with his closed fist, to keepe him off; which they call Butting, and place in weldoing the same, no small poynt of manhood.
>
> If hee escape the first, another taketh him in hand, and so a third, neyther is he left, untill ... hee eyther touch the ground with some part of his bodie, in wrastling, or cry, Hold; which is the word of yeelding. Then must he cast the ball (named Dealing) to some one of his fellowes, who catching the same in his hand, maketh away withall as before; and if his hap or agility bee so good, as to shake off or outrunne his counterwayters, at the goale, hee findeth one or two fresh men, readie to receive and keepe him off ...
>
> The hurlers are bound to the observation of many lawes as, that they must hurle man to man, and not two set upon one man at once: that the Hurler against the ball, must not but, nor hand-fast under

girdle: that hee who hath the ball, must but onely in the others brest: that he must deale no Fore-ball, viz. he may not throw it to any of his mates, standing neerer the goale, then himselfe ... These hurling-matches are mostly used at weddings, where commonly the guests undertake to encounter all commers.

The hurling to the Countrey, is bound to few of these orders: some two or more Gentlemen doe commonly make this match, appointing that on such a holyday, they will bring to such an indifferent place, two, three or more parishes of the East or South quarter, to hurle against so many other, of the West or North. Their goales are either those Gentlemens houses, or some townes or villages, three or four miles asunder ... a silver ball is cast up, and that company, which can catch, and carry it by force, or sleight, to their place assigned, gaineth the ball and victory.

The Hurlers take their next [nearest] way over hilles, dales, hedges, ditches; yea and thorow bushes, briers, mires, plashes and rivers whatsoever; so as you shall sometimes see 20. or 30. lie tugging together in the water, scrambling and scratching for the ball ... yea, there are horsemen placed also on either party (as it were in ambush) and ready to ride away with the ball, if they can catch it at advantage. But they may not so steale the palme: for gallop any one of them never so fast, yet he shall be surely met at some hedge corner, cross-lane, bridge, or deepe water, which they know he must needs touch at: and if his good fortune gard him not the better, hee is like to pay the price of his theft, with his owne and his horses overtthrowe to the ground.

Hurling in Cornwall, at its 'zenith in the later Middle Ages, declined through the 17th and 18th centuries in spite of attempts to popularise the game.'[10] *The Moderate Intelligencer* of May 4th 1654 records that one hundred Cornish gentlemen came up to London to give an exhibition of hurling in Hyde Park, 50 a side, one side in red caps, one in white. 'There was present his highness the Lord Protector, many of the Privy Council and divers eminent gentlemen, to whose view was presented great agility of body and most neat and exquisite wrestling which was ordered to show more the strength, vigour and nimbleness of their bodies than to endanger their persons. The ball they played withal was silver and designed for that party which did win the ball.' During the reign of Charles II, another great Cornish hurling match was staged in London and attracted thousands of spectators, among whom was the Duke of York. In the 19th century another exhibition match was played in Hyde Park in the 1820s.

The ancient game of hurling is now confined to the two parishes of St Columb Major and Minor, though attempts have been made to revive it in some other places. The game is a sort of extended football – the goals being the church towers of the contending parishes ... The prize is a silver ball, held by the winning parish until it is again played for 1879. *Murray's Hand-Book of Cornwall*

The game at St Columb Major is now played between Town and Country. Parishioners who live in the town are matched with those living in the rural parts of the parish. The goals consist of stone troughs standing by the roadside, each one mile from the centre of the town.

Wales

> I cannot overpasse a game used in on part of this sheere amonge the Welshmen both rare to heare, troblesome to discribe, and painefull to practise, yett for the rarieti thereof, I crave pardon to troble yow, and though somewhat longe, yett as breife as I maye, This game is called *Knappan* ... the game is thought to be of great antiquitie ... This Knappan happeneth and falleth out to be by two means, the on is a settled or standinge Knappan, the daie and place known and yeerelye observed, of these Knappan daies there were wont to be fyve in number ..., George Owen (1603), *The Description of Penbrokeshire*

These were Shrove Tuesday, Easter Monday, the Sunday after Easter, Ascension Day and Corpus Christi. On each of these days, one single pair of parishes played each other. These were near the western Pembrokeshire coast, but the last two were between Pembrokeshire and Cardiganshire men near Newcastle Emlyn.

> ... and thes ii last were the greate and mayne places farre exceedinge anye of the former in multitude of people for there hath often been esteemed two thousand foote beside horsemen ... And at these daies and places were these games wont yeerelye to be exercised without anye match makeinge or appointmente, and therefore I call these standinge Knappans. Appointed Knappans. The like playes would oftentymes be by makeinge of match between two gentlemen ... The gentlemen would devide the parishes, hundreds or sheres between them, and then ... intreate all his frindes and kinsmen in everye parishe to come and bringe his parishe wholelye with him ... there would alsoe resorte to the place diverse victualers with meate, drinke and wyne of all sortes, alsoe marchauntes, mercers and pedlers would provide stalls and boothes ... and for these causes some to playe, some to eate and drinke, some to buye, and some to sell, others to see and others to be seene (you know what kinde I mean) greate multitudes of people would resorte beside the plaiers. They contend not for anye wager or valuable thinge, but only for glorie and renowne, first for the fame of their Country in general, next every particular [individual] to wynne praise for his actyvitie and prowes ... Aboute one or two of the clocke afternoone begineth the playe, in this sorte, after a crye made both parties drawe together into some plaine, all first stripped bare, saveing a light paier of breeches, bare headed, bare bodied, bare leggs and feete ... for if he leave but his shirte on his back in the furye of the game yt is most commonly torn to peeces, and I have alsoe seene some longe locke gallantes trymely trymed at this game ... by pullinge theire haire and beardes ... the Barbor useth but his fistes and insteade of warme water taketh luke warme bludd, out of the nose, mouthe and face of the younker, this kind of trymeinge they all doe bestowe gratis without askinge anye thinge for theire paines.
> The foote companie thus meeting, there is a rounde bowle prepared of a reasonable quantitie, soe as a man may hold it in his hande and noe more, this bowle is of wood and should be boyled in tallow, for to make it slipperye and harde to be holden, this bowle is called Knappan,

and is by one of the companie hurld bolt upright to the ayre and at the fall, he that catcheth it hurleth it towared the countrey he playeth for, for gole ... there is non ... for the playe is not geven over untill the Knappan be soe farre carryed that there is no hope to returne it back that night, for the caryeinge of it a mile or two myles ... is no looseinge of the honor, soe it be still followed by the companie and the playe still maintained ... The Knappan beinge once caste furthe, you shall see the same tossed backwarde and forwarde, by hurling throwes, in strainge sorte, for in three or four throwes you shall see the whole bodie of the game removed, half a myle and more ... and it is a strange sight to see a thousand or fifteen hundred naked men to concurre together in a cluster in following the Knappan, as the same is hurled backewarde and forwarde ... The horsemen have monstrouse cudgells, of iii foote and a halfe longe, and he that thinketh himself well horsed maketh meanes to his ffrindes of the footmen to have the Knappan delivered him, which beinge gotten, he putteth spurres and awaye, as fast as the leggs will carrye, after him runneth the rest of the horsemen, and if they can overtake him, he sommoneth a deliverye of the Knappan; which should be thrise by lawe of the game, but now they scarce geve it once till he stricke, and if he hold the Knappan, yt is lawfull for the assaylante to beate him with his Cudgell, till he deliver it, the beste of foote troupes alsoe will followe the horse ... this exercise if due orders were observed, and the abuses reformed, were a most warlike exercise,both for horse and foote, but the disorders are so encreased that the playe is banished; and allmost forsaken, for by the Ancient custome of the playe, the footemen were not to use anye thinge, but the bare fistes, neyther was it permitted to the horsmen to come among the foote troupes, for that the footemen playeing all bare footed maye receave greate annoyance by the horse, and therefore it was permitted for the foote men to chase the horsemen from amonge them by hurling stones at them ... but now ... privatt grudges are revendged ...

As in Cornwall the game was often played on a Sunday which was anathema to Sabbatarians. The accidents occurring, as in Cornish hurling, and the violence that came with non-observance of the old rules were other factors in the discontinuance of Knappan.

Ireland

In the Celtic outer ring of Ireland, the Isle of Man and the Scottish Highlands hurling and shinty (and La Crosse in France) are related stick games. Hurling, the English, or rather Cornish, name for it, is one of Ireland's national games, confined to Irishmen both at home and abroad. It is the fastest of all field games. According to the ancient sagas and legends hurling existed before St Patrick's 5th-century conversion of the Irish to Christianity, the beginning of Irish written history. There are many references to it in the earliest manuscripts, and all Irish legendary heroes were skilled in the game.

Two centuries after the Anglo-Norman invasion of 1169, so many colonists were hurling that Edward III issued edicts against 'useless games which can be of no profit', on pain of imprisonment for those taking part 'in handball, football, cockfighting and hurling'. The

Statute of Galway in 1527 forbade the 'hurling of the little ball with hooked sticks or staves' and all other ball games which might threaten the practice of Archery 'except alone football with the grate ball'.

The Englishman John Dunton, poet and playwright, and book-seller in Dublin in 1698 has given a description of the game:

> I may say something to you of the sports used among the Irish on their holidays. One exercise they use much is their hurling ... When the cows are casting their hair, they pull it off their backs and with their hands work it into large balls which will grow very hard. This ball they use at the hurlings, which they strike with a stick called *commaan* and about three foot and a half long in the handle. At the lower end it is crooked and about three inches broad, and on this broad part you may sometime see one of the gamesters carry the ball tossing it for 40 or 50 yards in spite of all the adverse players; and when he is like to use it, he generally gives it a great stroke to drive it towards the goal.
>
> Sometimes if he miss his blow at the ball, he knocks one of the opposers down; at which no resentment is to be shown. They seldom come off without broken heads or shins in which they glory very much ... one parish sometimes or barony challenges another; they pick out ten, twelve, or twenty players of a side, and the prize is generally a barrel or two of ale, which is brought into the field and drunk off by the victors on the spot, though the vanquished are not without a share ... This commonly is upon some very large plain, the barer of grass the better and the goals are 200 or 300 yards one from the other; At some of these gatherings two thousand have been present together.

This is 'hurling to goals'. Much later, in the early 19th century, 'hurling home' became popular (though it was similarly doomed): all the men of neighbouring parishes, two or three hundred per side, set on hurling the ball home to their village across country.

> By the 18th century ... there were two ... distinct versions of the game. One was akin to modern field hockey, or shinty, in that it did not allow handling of the ball; it was played with a narrow, crooked stick; it used a hard wooden ball ...; it was mainly a winter game. This game, called *camán* (anglicised to 'commons') was confined to the northern half of the country ... The second version of the game (*iomán*) ... was of southern provenance. The ball could be handled or carried on the hurl, which was flat and round-headed; the ball ... was soft and made of animal hair; the game was played in summer. Unlike commons, this form of hurling was patronised by the gentry, as a spectator and gambling sport, associated with fairs and other public gatherings ...
>
> A number of factors determined the distribution of the southern game. The most important was the patronage of local gentry families ... They picked the teams, arranged the hurling greens and supervised the matches, which were frequently organised as gambling events. The southern hurling zone coincides with the area where, in the late medieval period, the Norman and Gaelic worlds fused to produce a vigorous culture ... It is closely linked to the distribution of big farms ... Landlord patronage was essential to the well-being of the southern game; once it was removed ... the game collapsed into shapeless anarchy ... As one hostile observer put it: A hurling match is a scene of drunkenness, blasphemy and all kinds and manners of debauchery

8. Hurling with the broad-bladed *iomán* or hurley 1853. The wide striking blade of the hurley allows the ball to be struck far and fast, overhead as well as along the ground. The wide blade also enables a player to run with the ball balanced or hopping on it. The ball may be kicked, caught before hitting, but not thrown nor carried, nor lifted from the ground by hand.

By the mid 19th century, hurling had declined so steeply that it survived in only three pockets, around Cork city, in south-east Galway and in the area north of Wexford town. Amongst the reasons for decline were ... political turbulence, sabbitudinarianism, modernisation and the dislocating impact of the Famine ...

'Rediscovery' usually involves an invention of tradition ... Thus, when Michael Cusack set about reviving the game, he codified a synthetic version ... modelled on the southern 'iomán' version that he had known as a child in Clare. Not surprisingly, this new game never caught on in the old 'commons' area, with the Glens of Antrim being the only major exception ... From the beginning the revived game had a nationalist veneer [and] depended on the active support of an increasingly nationalistic Catholic middle class ... Thus, hurling's early success was in south Leinster and east Munster, the very region which pioneered popular Irish nationalist politics ..., Kevin Whelan, 'The Geography of Hurling' in *History Ireland*, (Spring 1993)

Gaelic football is another national game peculiar to the Irish at home and abroad. Football was being played in the 14th century. The Gaelic Athletic Association codified the game in 1885, some years after Association and Rugby Union were invented. As nationalists, the GAA devised rules that were different from the British games. Gaelic football was chiefly played outside the main hurling area, in the wetter central region. It is now, in terms of numbers, even more

9. Shinty c. 1840 While the game with the narrow-bladed stick or *caman* finally died out in northern Ireland, it remained popular in the Scottish Highlands as Camanachd, more commonly known as Shinty or Shinny.

popular than hurling. Australian Rules Football, though played with an oval ball, is derived from Gaelic football, which was brought by the Irish in the gold-fields of Ballarat and Bendigo.

Scotland

In the 6th century, when most of northern Europe was overrun by heathen hordes, Ireland, which had escaped occupation by the invaders, as it had by the Romans, sent out missionaries to re-convert the peoples of Europe to Christianity. When invading Irish Gaels crossed the narrow water between Antrim and Argyll to set up a kingdom there, missionaries went with them. From there they brought the Word to the Pictish kingdoms of the Highlands and Islands; and, along with it, they took the Gaelic language and the *camán* hurling. While the game with the narrow-bladed stick finally died out in northern Ireland, it remained popular in the Highlands as Camanachd, now more commonly known as shinty or shinny.

In more modern times shinty survived Calvinist Sabbatarianism, the pacification of the Highlands (at Glencoe in 1692 the Campbells played shinty with the Macdonalds, before massacring them, at night), and Culloden (1746). By the mid-19th century the Highland Clearances and repressive Calvinism caused a decline, and shinty was played in only a few places. A modern revival followed the formation of the Camanachd Association in 1893, when the rules of the game were drawn up. The revival was supported by renewed interest in the universities. Today shinty is firmly established in its limited area.

Conclusion

It is perhaps idle to speculate whether football in England owes its origin to any of these games. In contrast to them, in England there is a lack of description of early football, significant perhaps of a lack of interest among the literate. If there is a debt, it must be to France. 'Almost everything that was a game, amusement or diversion in England was, in the Middle Ages, of Norman or Angevin origin.'[11] Yet La Soule was played, at least latterly, with a wooden *boule* or a ball filled with stuffing, and with limited use of the feet. A ball to be kicked, as the word foot-ball indicates, is best filled with air, as in Italy. Yet an air-ball would be quite inappropriate for the extremely rough treatment the ball received in La Soule; and its status as a prized object, whether of religious origin or not, would hardly stretch to a replacement, let alone to being pumped up in mid-game. On the other hand, it is quite possible that the Shrove Tuesday cross-country mass football games, between neighbouring villages or parishes, derive from France, since they do resemble La Soule. The English soldiers in France during the Hundred Years War would have witnessed such games. The earliest mention of Shrove Tuesday football in England (apart from that in 1174 in London) is as late as 1533 at Chester, though of course that does not mean that the game did not exist earlier.[12] These games are still played at a few places in England and the Scottish Borders, but records of them do not often go back beyond the late 18th century. It is probably safe to say that football in its modern forms has its origin in the temperate maritime lowlands of north-west Europe, where land and climate were most conducive to playing it.

The 19th century

By the early years of the 19th century, political and religious, as well as economic and social changes had all but put an end to football and associated games everywhere. A vital factor in the continuance of a game had been the involvement in it of the ruling or landed classes. But for a variety of reasons, by the 19th century that involvement was withdrawn. In Italy native rulers gave way to Austrians, who had no interest in Calcio. The resentment of the French peasantry at the seigneurial *droit de soule* effectively ended the game at the Revolution. In Wales and Ireland the landed gentry withdrew support when their games became debased by extreme violence and debauchery; Cornish hurling, more gentlemanly, lasted longer, though never on a Sunday.

England avoided the political upheavals of the Continent with their consequent brake on the diversions of the upper classes. Hunting, shooting, fishing and cricket continued unabated in the 19th century, along with horse-racing and, for a time, bare-knuckle boxing, both of which attracted the national indulgence for betting.

The only exception (proving the rule) was the form of football known as *camping* or *camp-ball*, confined to East Anglia, the old Danelaw. The name is supposedly derived from the Anglo-Saxon kemp or camp, one who combats hand to hand.

> *Camping*, though not so general, is still a favourite exercise in some districts of both our counties. The late Right honourable William Wyndham, scarcely more celebrated as a statesman and a philosopher, than as a patron of the 'Sports and Pastimes of the English People', on a principle truly patriotic, though it might sometimes incur ridicule, gave great encouragement to this sport during his residences in the country, and had many matches in the neighbourhood of his venerable seat at Felbrigg. He was wont to say, that it combined all athletic excellence; that to excel in it, a man must be a good boxer, runner and wrestler; in short a sort of pancratiast ...[13] The late Lord Rochford was also a great patron of this sport in the neighbourhood of his seat at Easton in Suffolk ... Two varieties are at present expressly recognised; ·ough-play and civil-play. In the latter there is no boxing. [In both versions] two goals are pitched at the distance of 120 yards from each other. The number in each side is very commonly twelve, R. Forby (1830), *The Vocabulary of East Anglia*

In rough-play the numbers were often in the hundreds. Areas set aside for playing, known as camping-land, camping– close or camping-pightle, are mentioned in 15th-century documents, and these same names are found on modern maps. Forby's description of the game tells a familiar story:

> The contest for the ball begins, and never ends without black eyes and bloody noses, broken heads or shins, and some serious mischiefs. If the ball can be, carried, kicked or thrown to one of the goals ... it is reckoned one towards the game ...
>
> [In the 18th century there was] a celebrated camping, Norfolk against Suffolk, on Diss Common, with 300 on each side. Before the ball was thrown up, the Norfolk side enquired tauntingly of the Suffolk men, if they had brought their coffins. The Suffolk men after 14 hours were the victors. Nine deaths were the result of the contest within a fortnight. These were called fighting camps, for much boxing was practised in them.[14]

In 1822 at a camp between Happing and Blofield Hundreds at Ranworth there were 6000 spectators. The last recorded camp took place in 1831 on Norwich Cricket Ground.

Chapter 2

The Public Schools

Sports at the Old Public Schools

The many hundreds of ancient Endowed Grammar Schools all over England were founded for the education of local boys. In course of time, maybe, they acquired a few paying boarders from further afield to augment the schoolmaster's fixed stipend, if the trustees agreed, and if he had room for them in his house. The usher to teach the younger boys was his only assistant. What his pupils did outside the schoolroom was of small concern to the schoolmaster. His school was for learning Latin Grammar and perhaps a little Greek, not for field sports or for playing games. The teaching of Latin was often laid down in a school's statutes, and long remained essential learning for a career in the law or the church, the traditional avenues of advancement.

During the late 17th and the 18th centuries the great majority of the Grammar Schools were in decline, eventually becoming 'decayed'. The narrowness of the classical syllabus had become inappropriate as a training for very many occupations and this was one reason for decline. Another reason often was the fall in value of the original endowment of a school, which meant that it could no longer attract a good schoolmaster. Some schools disappeared, some became elementary schools.

During the 18th century thousands of small Private Schools, however, offered an alternative and altogether more modern curriculum. Many of them were Dissenting Academies run by nonconformists disqualified from office in Grammar Schools after the Restoration – a further reason for their decline. Middle-class parents were prepared to pay the owner for providing a more modern and practical curriculum of reading English, handwriting, arithmetic, French and accounts.

In contrast, for a handful of these endowed Grammar Schools the 18th century was largely a very successful period. They had become boarding-schools, the so-called Public Schools: Winchester (1382), Eton (1440), Westminster (1560), Harrow (1571), Charterhouse (1611), and the two schools north of London, Shrewsbury (1552) and Rugby (1567). They had turned themselves into public (as opposed to local) schools by increasing the number of assistant masters and by acquiring from elsewhere in the country fee-paying, respectively, Commoners, Oppidans, Town Boys, Foreigners who boarded in masters' houses or in lodgings in the town. During the 18th century, with improved coach travel on turnpike roads, the aristocracy and gentry began to send their sons to board at these few schools in increasing numbers. Eventually these non-local pupils far outnumbered the free Foundationers (respectively Scholars, Collegers, Gownboys) of the original foundation.

Winchester and Eton differed from the others, not only in antiquity, but also (like the 17th century Charterhouse) in being boarding schools from the outset. William of Wykeham, Bishop of Winchester, and, following his example, Henry VI for practical ecclesiastical reasons wished to promote book-learning among the illiterate noble and knightly classes. In addition to the poor scholars of the foundation who lived in College (Collegers), a few young aristocrats were admitted (commensales) who paid for their board, or 'commons', and lodged in the town (Commoners at Winchester, Oppidans at Eton). At Winchester they ate at the Fellows' table. Other, less exalted Commoners, ate with the scholars.

The other 'public' schools were similarly reformed. Westminster, founded by Henry VIII, was re-founded by Elizabeth after her sister Mary had restored the Abbey to a monastery. It was governed by the Dean and Chapter. Charterhouse was founded by Thomas Sutton, an Elizabethan captain, who turned the old Carthusian monastery at Smithfield into a hospital for impoverished officers and a grammar school for sons of poor gentlemen who had served on land or sea (Gownboys). Shrewsbury was started by the bailiffs and burgesses (the Corporation) of the town, under a Charter of Edward VI, with later amendment by Elizabeth I. Under Elizabeth it flourished with four or five hundred boys from a wide catchment area. Unlike the other public schools, the 18th century was a period of decline for Shrewsbury. Numbers fell to a mere eighteen in 1798, after which Dr Samuel Butler (1798-1836), the school's first non-Salopian headmaster, revived its fortunes swiftly and dramatically. Harrow and Rugby, like Charterhouse, were founded by philanthropic laymen, less grand than episcopal Winchester and royal Eton and Westminster: at Harrow, John Lyon, and at Rugby, Lawrence Sheriff. Harrow was a small country grammar school initially, but in the 18th century its closeness to London, the patronage of the Whig nobility (opposed to Tory Eton) and a succession of great headmasters resulted in its replacing Westminster as Eton's main rival. Rugby's late reincarnation as a public school was the work of Dr James (1778-94) who in the last quarter of the 18th century raised numbers from 52 to 245, aided by a rich windfall when leases fell in on land in Gray's Inn Fields on the outskirts of London, the endowment of Lawrence Sheriff.

*

Boys of these seven boarding-schools, benefitting from their abundant free-time, played a major part in developing team sports and in promoting competitive matches in the first half of the 19th century. Their influence expanded when they went up to Oxford and Cambridge, where together, for a time, they formed the majority of undergraduates.

The term 'public school' is not found before the 18th century. By the end of that century, however, the distinction between the small group of public schools and the rest of the grammar schools was well established, although membership of the group, outside the permanent core of Eton, Winchester and Westminster, was often in dispute. In 1816 Rudolph Ackermann (the printmaker) published his illustrated history of the principal schools of England, inconclusively entitled *History of the Public Schools &c. &c.* He omitted Shrewsbury and included the London day schools St Paul's (1509) and Merchant Taylors' (1561) as well as a fifth London school, Christ's Hospital (1592), which unlike its fellows had remained an entirely charitable establishment.

In 1820 the Whig M.P., Henry (later Lord) Brougham introduced his Endowed Schools Bill to enquire into the administration, or maladministration, of their ancient charitable endowments. One clause proposed that English reading, writing and accounts should be added to the curriculum, and another that the taking of boarders should be limited or even forbidden. Tory political pressure forced the exclusion from the Bill of the public schools. Samuel Butler wrote to the Hon. H.G.Bennet, M.P.:

> Writing to you on a previous occasion I claimed that Shrewsbury School should be put on at least as favourable a footing as Eton, Westminster or any other. I now see that in this Bill Eton, Westminster and Winchester, Harrow, Charterhouse and Rugby are excepted as being public schools. I claim the same exception for Shrewsbury ... and I beg to state my reasons.
>
> If by a public school is meant one to which persons from all parts of the kingdom send their sons for education ... and I cannot conceive any other meaning of the term ... then I beg leave to say that there is now and usually have been during my mastership boys at Shrewsbury from almost every county in England and Wales, some from Scotland and some from Ireland ... There are more prizemen at Cambridge from Shrewsbury School in proportion to numbers than any other school in England.

As the Bill never passed into law the threat to Shrewsbury's outstanding classical scholarship – the achievement of Samuel Butler himself – and to its existence as a boarding school were averted.

But this small group of schools continued to be recognised as the public schools for many years after other boarding schools were founded in mid-century or were developed from existing grammar schools. Their status was later acknowledged by the Public Schools Act of 1868 which followed the Report of the Clarendon Commission. Clarendon had enquired into the finances, administration, studies etc. of nine schools, Eton, Winchester, Westminster, Charterhouse,

10. Winchester College from the north. The Chapel's east window and the Hall steps are shown by making them face north. Wykeham's original belfry was taken down in 1474. The College was founded for a Warden, 10 fellows, 70 scholars, 3 Chaplains, 3 Lay Clerks, 16 Choristers and 2 Masters. All 105 are shown in this first Public School group picture. In addition to the 70 Scholars and 16 Choristers the Statutes allowed for 10 sons of the nobility who, as Commoners, lived out, sitting at the Fellows' table for meals. Shortly afterwards other day-boys were taken in who sat at the Scholars' table. A couple of Fellows' Commoners are seen in a joust in the outer court, and one of them is unhorsed. The larger figure is probably a beggar, to indicate the charitable status of the College.

St Paul's, Merchant Taylors', Harrow, Rugby and Shrewsbury. The Report made many criticisms and some recommendations. By the Act the old restrictive statutes were set aside and new governing bodies were constituted which were required to submit new statutes within a given time. The two London day schools governed by City Livery Companies were exempted from these measures.

Early Sport at Winchester and Eton

With its 70 scholars Winchester (1382) was the first school with a large number of boarders, and hence was the first to experience the need to provide space for their physical activities. The Statutes, published in 1400, include no mention of a playground. Within the college there was limited space, but a mile and a half away is St Catharine's Hill, which at least from the 16th century, and possibly earlier, was where the scholars had to climb to take their exercise on whole holidays, and on half-holidays. Permission for the latter was granted by the Warden in response to the Head Boy's request, and the period of leave was known as a 'remedy'. On these days (Tuesdays and Thursdays) they went up to 'Hills' twice, once before breakfast and again at half-past two under the supervision of prefects. These excursions were the only occasions until the 19th century, apart from visits to the Cathedral, when the scholars were allowed out of the college.

The various Latin-English phrase books used for teaching at Winchester provide most of the evidence for the continuous playing of games from at least the 15th century as well as of schoolmasterly support for them. William Horman entered Winchester in 1468 and returned as its headmaster in 1495, having spent ten years as headmaster of Eton. In his collection of sentences, *Vulgaria*, published in 1519, there is a section on games which reflects the recreations of his boys:

He caste away his gowne lest it shulde lette hym of his rennynge.
Children do lerne to swymme lenying upon the rynde of a tree or corke.
I have wrasteled and runne: and I have hadde the worse at both games:

He is a royal coyter [*Est egregius discobolas*]
He made a iustynge with speris.
He roweth his bote ageynst the streme.
Fet me myn anglynge rodde: with a bayted hooke.
It is a shame that a yonge gentylman shulde lose tyme at the dyce and tabuls
[backgammon] cardis and hasarde.
Let me have the red chesse men.
I have bought a pleying tabull: with XII poynts [squares] on the one syde and
chekkers on the other syde.
My cocke had the best in this fyght.
I have thrown a stone over the house.

Archery was played as a sport rather than a duty, as the scholars were destined to enter the priesthood:

I cannot bend my bowe: yet he is weke.
Whatever he marketh with his yie he smyteth with his arowe.
The maister of the game gave me a sylver arowe.

Tennis is the only ball game that is quoted:

> Thou playest featly [elegantly] at the tynis: and very quyuerly [agilely].
> A tenys player [spherista] assayeth all the joynt of his body.
> He hyt me in the yie with a tenys balle.
> Tenys playenge [spheromachia] hath hurt many men.
> I have left my boke in the tenys playe [*pilatorio*].*
> I will play with the at tenys hande to hande.**
> We will pley with a ball full of wynde.***

In *Vulgaria* Horman has some advice for schoolmasters:

> Give thy scolars some recreation from theyr books.
> Many remedies make easy scolars.
> There must be a measure in gyunge of remedies [remissionibus] or sportynge to chyldren: lest they be wery of goynge to theyr boke if they have none: or waxe slacke if they have to many.
> Some children be well ruled for love: some for fere: some not without bettynge or correction.

All the games mentioned by Horman in 1519 were suitable diversions for one or for two individuals. None were team games, and few would have been played on 'Hills'. In his Latin themes Christopher Johnson, a Winchester boy from 1549-53 and headmaster from 1560-71, makes the first mention of St Catharine's Hill as a playground:

> ... nothing new for some to shirk Hills at playtime.

He complains:

> What forgetful, unskilled, ignorant, thick, clumsy dolts you are! If when your books are shut up all you can do is play, then you may not shut up your books![1]

Robert Matthews in his Latin poem, written while a boy at Winchester in 1647, says of going to 'Hills':

> Here you learn to excel at throwing the quoit, or you enjoy playing at tennis [*pila palmaria*], and often you like to strike the ball with ringing bat or kick it with your feet. To play these innocent games is permitted, with others which I will not mention.

This is the first mention of football and an early form of cricket, games for a number of boys which could only be played on 'Hills' and

---

*   Probably a walled court without a roof.

**   Hand tennis was still the custom at the start of the 16th century. In 1506 Henry VII watched a tennis match where 'the King of Castile played with the Racket and gave the Marquess of Dorset XV'.

***   It is significant that Horman does not feel it necessary to translate the word *pugillari* in his Latin example – of or belonging to a fist or hand – which describes the play, an indication that air balls were then for hands only, and not for feet.

11. 'Hills' was St Catherine's Hill, a mile and a half from College. 'About 500 feet high, and near the top surrounded by a deep trench, the remains of an old Roman camp. The boys had to ascend twice a day on whole holidays and Remedies [games days], once before breakfast, and again at half-past-two'. Each boy had to walk with a socius (companion) when going to Hills or the Cathedral, in the mid-19th century wearing his 'cathedral hat'. 'We march forth each (as on our way back) with a socius, till we reach the hill-top. There must be no going outside 'trench' which confines the hill like a girdle, no sitting on the ground, for that spells fever. Often you like to strike the ball with ringing bat or to kick it with your feet. To play these innocent games is permitted.' Robert Mathew's Latin poem c. 1647. 'Our cricket matches were played in Meads – but the first Junior match of the season was always played at the top of Hills when the heroic player might sometimes hit a Trencher, or even one to go over the Trench, in which case it would roll on for ever. (W.A.Fearon *Passing of Old Winchester*, 1852-9). In 1868 Dr Ridding issued the order 'that there should be no Hills', and so it came to an end.

not near college buildings. In 1790, long after the college had acquired meadowland adjoining it, a playground was at last provided, for the Scholars only, in 'Meads'; but the arduous climb up to 'Hills' continued until ended by the headmaster in 1868. By this time 'the development of cricket and football had already made "going on Hills" unfashionable'.

Henry VI had stayed at Winchester many times, and he took it as his model when founding Eton in 1440. The Statutes are similar, and on Eton's foundation not only Winchester's headmaster, but half of the fellows and half of the scholars were transferred there. So it can be assumed that Winchester's system of provision for games was followed from the start. The King bought up as much land in Eton for his school as he could, so that the current playing fields had been acquired by 1443. The first expenditure for recreation, however, appears in the accounts only in the early 16th century.

As at Winchester there is no mention in the statutes of what games were to be played, only a prohibition of specific activities.

No one shall keep in the College any hounds, nets, ferrets, hawks or falcons for sport; nor any monkeys, bears, foxes, deer, badgers or any unusual and rare wild beasts, such as would be unprofitable or dangerous to the College. There shall be no jumping or wrestling, throwing of stones or balls, lest damage be done to the walls or windows.

William Horman, who returned to Eton as a fellow in 1502, includes in his *Vulgaria* 'The tems is over the bankis'. He included, furthermore, many examples of fishing. These and references to swimming and boating come, in all probability, from Eton rather than Winchester.

Tennis

Pila palmaria (cf. French *paume*) on 'Hills' was the simpler version of tennis, played without walls. The only equipment needed was a ball. The exact location of the walled tennis court is not known. But in 1640 the Bursars' Accounts show expenditure 'for restoring the walls of the cloister which are in disrepair, and renovating the holes in the walls around the old Sphaeristerium ...' In 1768 a net was purchased which indicates tennis was still being played. The rules of the game were codified in France in 1592, but it is probable that Winchester had worked out its own set of rules.

The Eton Audit Book of 1600-1 reads: 'Item to Giles mending the ... Tennys court walls', and 1602-3: 'iii daies tiling the Tennis courte'. A roof has been put on what had previously been a walled rectangle open to the sky (unless it was a re-tiling job). In July 1776 'A boy high up in the school describes himself as taking no amusement except tennis.' However scant the evidence, it is clear that tennis was the first popular ball game played at England's two oldest boarding schools, probably from the 15th to the 18th centuries.

During the 16th and 17th centuries Tennis was very popular at the Universities, the destination of the Winchester and Eton scholars. At Cambridge tennis, bowls and archery were the only permitted sports. Ten of the sixteen colleges had a tennis court, four-walled and mostly unroofed. At Oxford too the majority of colleges had a ball court, but they differed in appearance from those at Cambridge, the most advanced having three and a half walls, more like fives courts in appearance, and possibly in use too; other courts had two walls, built high, at right angles. Like the word 'fives', 'tennis' had a wide variety of interpretations.

*

The origins of tennis at public schools lie in France. The royal game of La Paume from which most modern court games derive, was played in French castles and monastery cloisters from the 12th century. It was played over a line on the ground or over a cord with or without a net attached, at first with the palm of the hand and later

12b. Tennis Court at Emmanuel College, Cambridge

12a. Tennis Court at St John's College, Cambridge

12c. Ball Court at Merton College, Oxford

Tennis / Ball Courts at Cambridge (1688) and Oxford (1675) by David Loggan. Some of the Cambridge courts were roofed, some open, or roofed or open at different times. The courts shown here at St John's and Emmanuel Colleges are the *jeu quarré* variety without dedans or penthouse above it, but with two hazards in the wall, *le petit trou* below and the wooden board (*l'ais*) above. At Oxford the ball-courts consisted of two heightened walls at right-angles as at Merton, or three and a half-sided courts with a buttress, more like Fives courts in appearance, and possibly in use. Like the word 'Fives', 'Tennis' had a wide interpretation.

12d. Ball Court at University College, Oxford

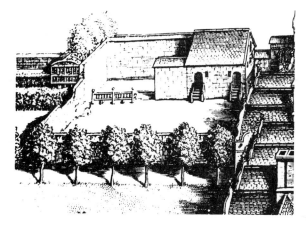

12e. Ball Court (and Necessarium) at Oriel College, Oxford

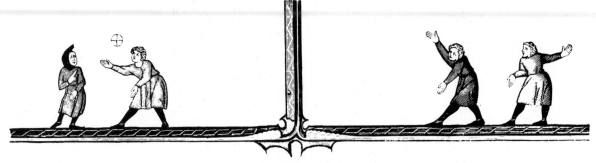

13. Tennis. From a 14th century illuminated manuscript of a French Romance *Histoire de Lancelot ou S. Graal*. The dividing line is not a net, but part of an inter-columnar ornament, probably intended to indicate a line on the ground.

with a racket. It was played in the open as *longue paume* or in an enclosed space as *courte* (short) *paume*. *Longue paume*, the older game, was played in dry castle moats, or in open fields, parks, quadrangles and streets. It is a predecessor of lawn tennis, and also developed into *pelota* in Spain and *pallone* in Italy. In *courte paume* the shape of the enclosed court depended on the configuration of its surroundings before a standard court was adopted. It is the most ancient court game still being played, and to some people it is still the best. Our word 'court' comes from *courte paume*. The French called the place where it was played a *jeu*, whether for *courte* or *longue paume*.

> The game was called 'royal', and not without cause. Capetians, Valois and Bourbons had handed down, along with the crown, the love of this exercise. Francois I (1515-1547) was very skilled at it, and so was his son, Henri II, who had a magnificent *salle* built for the game at the Louvre ... From the beginning of the 16th century the racket prevailed, although some players still continued to hit the ball with their hand ...[2]

La Paume was exceptional in that women competed against men.

> In [1427] or a little earlier, came to Paris a woman called Margot, quite young, about 28 to 30 years old, who was of the county of Hainault, and played better at hand-ball than any man had seen; and with that she played both fore-handed and back-handed [*et avec ce jouoit devant main derrière main*] very powerfully, very cunningly, and very cleverly, as any man would, and there were but few men whom she did not beat, except the very best players, and it was the Court in Paris where the best play was, in the Rue Grenier Saint Lazare, which was called the Petit-Temple (From a private diary kept during the reigns of Charles VI and VII, September 5, 1427.)

At hand-ball one can play with right and left hand, but it is hardly likely that this lady, a contemporary of Jeanne d'Arc, would have used the back of her hand and possibly she was playing with a racket.

> In 1592 the rules of the game were codified in France ... The number of *jeux de paume* built in the 16th and 17th centuries is amazing: not a château which did not have its own, and not a city that did not possess ten or so; even small towns had theirs ... Francesco Gregory

14. Frontispiece of a book containing the first laws of the game known to exist. The court became a theatre like most of the courts of the 17th century.

d'Ierni, who accompanied the papal legate to Paris in 1596, found there, 250 *jeux de paume*, very fine, and very well established, which, I am told, before the recent wars provided a living for 7000 people' (janitors, *maitres de jeux*, markers – who were also employed to rub

15. The Interior of a Jeu de Paume. This picture appears in a treatise by Francois de Garsault, *Art du paumier-raquetier et de la paume*, published in Paris in 1767. He describes two kinds of court or *jeu*. The one shown here is *le jeu à dedans*, with penthouse roof on three sides and the dedans for spectators (with protective netting omitted). This is the Tennis court in use today. The other court was *le jeu quarré* with no dedans, or penthouse above it, but with hazards in the wall. This can be seen in the pictures of Cambridge courts.

down the players after the matches, owners of the court, and makers of balls and rackets, etc.)[3]

Henri IV ('Paris is worth a Mass') was a constant player.

The King played *la paume* the whole of the afternoon in the *Jeu de la Sphère* with M. d'O ... Saturday 24th of the same month, the King played the whole day at la paume ... He was stripped to his shirt, and it was torn all down the back, and he wore grey breeches, called *jambes de chien*, and was so tired that he could not get to the ball and he said he was like an ass because he failed in the feet. Friday 16th September 1594, the day after his entry into Paris, (*Journal du Règne de Henri IV*, Pierre l'Estoille, Henri IV's *grand audiencier*.)

Sir Robert Dallington was a visitor to the France of Henri IV. He was later to become the Master of Charterhouse (1624-37). In his often critical book *A Method of Travel Showed by Taking View of France as it Stood in the Year 1598* (London, 1604) he writes of:

Their Exercises
I am now by order to speeke of their Exercises wherein, methinks, the Frenchman is very immoderate, especially in those which are somewhat violent; for ye may remember, ye have seene them play Sets of Tennise in the heat of summer, & height of the day, when others were scarce able to stirre out of dores. This immoderate play in this unseasonable time, together with their intemperate drinking and feeding, is the onely cause, that heere ye see them generally itchy and scabbed, some of them in so foule a sort, as they are unfit for any honest table ... Tennis Play As for the exercise of Tennis play, which I above remembred, it is more here used, then in all Christendome besides; whereof may witnesse the infinite number of Tennis Courts throughout the land, insomuch as yee cannot finde that little Burgade, or

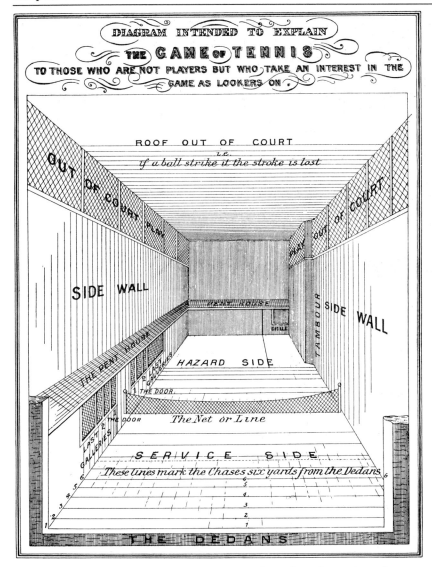

16. Scoring is similar to lawn tennis. The service, always from the service end, must bounce off the side wall penthouse on the hazard (receiver's) end on to the service court, beyond the chase lines. A point is scored by hitting the ball into the grille or the last (winning) gallery on the hazard side, or into the dedans on the service side. A point is lost if the ball is hit out of court, into the net, or into a gallery on the player's own side of the net. The receiver also loses a point if the ball bounces twice (off any wall) in the rear area of the court. If the ball bounces twice on the lined area on either side of the net, or enters an opposite gallery, a chase is called. The point is neither won nor lost, but is held in abeyance until game point, or a second chase, when ends are changed. This is the only way for service to change. In the rallies following, the player who allowed the ball to bounce twice must try to make a chase better than his opponent has done, that is make the second bounce nearer the back of the court, to win the point. Thus the ball needs to be hit to a length. If hit too short, it may be left to bounce twice. If hit too long, it rebounds from the back wall and can be easily returned. So the chase helps to determine the real tennis stroke, a downward-chopping stroke, from the elbow, that cuts the ball.

towne in France, that hath not one or moe of them. Here are, as you see, three score in Orleans, and I know not how many hundred there be in Paris: but of this I am sure, that if there were other places the like proportion, ye should have two Tennis Courts, for every one Church through France. Methinks it is also strange how apt they be here to play well, that ye would thinke they were borne with Rackets in their hands, even the children themselves manage them so well, and some of their women also, as we observed at Blois. There is one great abuse in this exercise, that the Magistrates do suffer every poore Citizen, and Artificer to play thereat, who spendeth that on the Holy-day at Tennis, which hee got the whole weeke, for the keeping of his poore family. A thing more hurtfull then our Ale-houses in England, though the one the other be bad enough. And of this I dare assure you, that of this sort of poore people, there be more Tennis Players in France, then Ale-drinkers, or Malt-wormes (as they call them) with us. [In fact there were various royal ordinances against the common people playing courte paume in the jeux de paume, regularly issued and regularly ignored.] You observe here that their Balles are of cloth, which fashion they have held this seven yeares: before which time they were of lether, like ours. Much more may be made of this exercise, but I will not reade you a Lecture in the Schoole of Tennis, whom I confesse the better Scholler.

Everywhere in France in the 16th and 17th centuries courts also served as theatres, and this held back new theatre design. While elsewhere in Europe from the 16th century theatres were built in the form of a semi-circle, in France, even in the 18th century, the shape of a *jeu de paume* was retained.

> The 16th century was the golden age of the *jeu de paume* ... By the end of the 18th century the game was in full decadence. The decline had even begun from the time of Louis XIV (1643-1715); the king played it, but without passion ... In 1657 the Dutch ambassador counted still 114 courts in Paris; in 1780 there were no more than 10; in 1839 only one ... which disappeared that year. Another succeeded it, which still remains, more exactly two, on the terrace of the Tuileries [in 1901. These courts were built by order of Napoleon III].[4]

The owners of the *jeux de paume* had found it more profitable to hire them out to theatre companies, rather than to players of the game; and adjustments were made to the interior of the buildings. On 19 June 1789 the *Tiers État* assumed the name of *Assemblée Nationale*. Louis XVI closed the doors of their chamber. On the next day the deputies met in the privately owned *jeu de paume* at Versailles and took their 'Oath of the Tennis Court', which marked the start of the French Revolution. 'That famous day was the first of the immortality of the Tennis Court at Versailles, and the last of its prosperity'.[5] With its royal and noble patrons dead or in exile the game in France was virtually at an end.

La Paume was also played in Italy, Spain, Germany and England. In Italy, Antonio Scaino da Salò in his *Trattato del giuoco della palla* (Treatise on the Game of Ball) published in Venice in 1555, describes

six different games of 'Tennis' in 71 chapters (and Calcio/football in one final one). Pallone was a large ball of 12 inch diameter pumped up with air. It was played in the open between two sides of three players, divided by a line on the ground. The ball was struck by a gauntlet or arm-piece in the form of a wooden cylinder with spikes, covering the lower forearm, with a grip for the hand. Scanno was a guitar-shaped club narrowing to where it was held in the hand; it used a smaller air-ball.

These two games were classified as arm-ball. The four other games were the Italian versions of Long and Short Paume, played with hand or with racket. The only games in a walled court and with dividing net were the short Paume ones, Palla della Corda. Originally there was just a cord, before a net the width of a hand was attached to it, to better judge whether the ball went over or under. The only difference between the French and Italian games mentioned by Scaino is that the Italians treated a 'net-cord' as a point lost, whereas the French regarded it as particularly skilful play. The small ball was filled either with wool or with air. The racket was very like to-day's Real Tennis racket, and because of expense was often replaced by a wooden bat with circular head (like a squash racket) or by a square one.

The game of Paume must have crossed the Channel by the 15th century. In 1414, at any rate, the Dauphin made a gift of tennis balls to Henry V.

When Philip, Archduke of Austria, by right of his wife Joana, daughter of Isabella of Castile, became King of that country, he left the Nether-

17. A tennis court at the Duke of Württemberg's New College at Tübingen, Engraved c. 1569. In Germany in the 16th century there was a Ballhaus in at least forty-six towns. 'Note the little standard, A, in the hand of the marker, which he placed at the point at which a chase was made and marked on the floor ... the marking of the chase by numbers on the wall and floor was not yet usual ... a peculiar hazard, marked B in each end-wall of the Court, which corresponds perhaps to the lune, mentioned in the old set of rules published in France'. Julian Marshall (1878) *The Annals of Tennis.*

18. *above* 16th-century *Pallone* in Italy. A *pallone* was a large ball of 12 inch diameter pumped up with air. It was played in the open between two sides of three players, divided by a line on the ground. The ball was struck by a gauntlet or arm-piece in the form of a wooden cylinder with spikes, covering the lower forearm, with a grip for the hand.

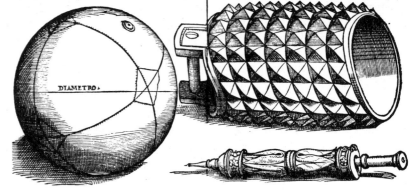

19. From *Trattato del giuoco della palla* by Antonio Scaino published in 1555. The large ball *pallone* measured 12 inches in diameter. It was made of three layers, each of eight pieces of untanned goatskin sewn together. The pump pushed air through the valve, also of goatskin, and the pressure of air inside the ball kept the internal tongue of the valve tight closed. (It was not until 1862 in Britain that the internal animal bladder was replaced by a rubber one and the broken off stem of a clay pipe and human lung-power gave way to a metal pump.) The armpiece was made of one piece of wood. The spikes gave greater control and produced 'cut' on the ball. *Scanno*, a less popular game, used a smaller ball, under 3 inches in diameter.

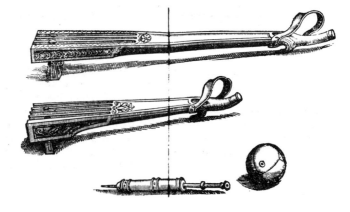

THE HIGH BORNE PRINCE IAMES DVKE OF YORKE
borne October = the 13. 1633.

M.Merian f.

20. The future James II. A keen Tennis player; he spent his exile at St Germain where there was a Jeu de Paume. He also played Golf and took part in the first international match, with a partner, against two English noblemen at the Scottish court. In the picture are a crowded dedans and two hazards in the wall below it. An ususual court, a *jeu quarré* with a *dedans*.

lands in the beginning of 1506 to take possession of his throne. The weather, however, was unfavourable, and he was compelled to seek shelter in the Port of Falmouth. Henry VII hearing that he was there, sent the Earl of Arundel and 'many more lords and knights' to attend him, and to bring him to Windsor, where he entertained him splendidly for many days, and whence he only allowed him to depart when he had obtained his signature to a very valuable treaty '... and then played the Kynge of Casteele with the Lord Marques of Dorset, the King lookynge one them, but the Kynge of Castelle played with the Rackete and gave the Lord Marques XV '.[6]

Here we find the hand still the usual implement of the English players, and the racket chosen, as if from habit, by a foreigner.[7]

Henry VII was, himself, a good player. His son, Henry VIII, built the court at Hampton Court Palace, which is still in use. Judging by the money he paid out in lost wagers, he was not too skilled. Elizabeth I was a keen spectator. James VI & I in his *Basilikon Doron* (1599), in contrast to his advice on football, recommends 'tennise' as suitable for his 6-year-old son, Prince Henry, advising him to use it and other sports moderately, 'not making a craft of them'. Charles I played at Oxford, where most colleges had a court, when the city was his stronghold in the Civil War; his son Charles II built a court in Whitehall Palace. He was seen by Samuel Pepys carefully weighing himself after a game, with the result that he found he had lost four and a half pounds. The game was as Royal (Real) in England as it was in France.

As with many outdoor field games, the restricted court games died when upper-class support disappeared. La Paume began its decline under an uncommitted Louis XIV and was finished off by the Revolution. In Italy Pallone succeeded Calcio as the leading game, but it too died when the nobility lost interest after Italian Reunification.[8] In England the Hanoverians did not follow the example of their Stuart predecessors.

Games at 16th-century Schools

Winchester and Eton were founded as boarding schools where games assumed much more importance than they did at day grammar schools.

At Shrewsbury and Harrow, and no doubt at other of the many grammar schools founded in the 16th century, Henry VIII's Act of 1541 for the Maintaining Artillery and Debarring of Unlawful Games was obeyed to the letter. At Shrewsbury the Bailiffs' Ordinances of 1577 directed that

> The scholars shall play only on Thursday, unless there be a holy-day in the week, or at the earnest request of some man of honour or of great worship credit or authority'. Their play was to be 'shooting in the long bow, and chess play and no other games unless it be running, wrestling, or leaping'. It is further provided that on every Thursday 'before they go to play the Scholars shall for exercise declaim and play one act of a [Latin] comedy.[9]

At Harrow the Orders, Statutes & Rules of John Lyon in 1590 direct that 'The scholars shall not be permitted to play except upon Thursday only sometimes when the weather is fine, and upon Saturday, or half-holidays after evening prayer. And their play shall be to drive a

top, toss a handball, to run, or to shoot, and none other.' Their parents
were instructed that:

> You shall allow your child at all times a bow, three shafts, bow-strings
> and a bracer to exercise shootings.

Pierce Egan in his *Book of Sports & Mirror of Life* of 1832 states that
'Archery, as a branch of school amusements, existed within the last
sixty years' at Harrow, but with increased numbers from the introduction of boarders and the demise of the long bow as a weapon of
war, it was probably not long before the boys at both schools filled
their leisure time with a variety of games. Originally, the only
playground at Harrow was the School Yard. Even there

> None above the First Form shall speak English in the School or when
> they are together at play. And for that and other faults, also let there
> be two Monitors.

In 1682 an orchard adjoining was levelled as a playing area, and
another field was added in 1750.

At Westminster by the Acts of the Dean and Chapter of Westminster 1563 it was decreed that

> There shall be no playing days granted to the scholars of the school but
> one day every week, and that to be on the Wednesday or Thursday
> only, and the same to be granted by the Dean, or in his absence by the
> sub-dean and Schoolmaster.

There was no specific mention of what games should or should not be
played by the 40 Queen's Scholars.

The Scholars were soon outnumbered by a variety of non-Founda-
tioners: Pensioners, who boarded in the school, Peregrines from
outside London, who lived with relatives or friends, and Oppidans
who lived at home.

Tothill Fields, the area of marshland now corresponding to Pimlico
and Belgravia, in the 17th century became a playground for Londoners. 'Because The Fields belonged to and were administered by the
Dean and Chapter, Westminster boys acquired the status of privileged users, and even had a skating pond specially dug for them.'[9]
The river provided some opportunity for boating.

From 1567 to 1748 Rugby was confined to its school-room in the
centre of the town. In the *Gentleman's Magazine* of September 1809
an Old Rugbeian who had been at the school in the 1740s wrote: 'I do
not recollect any playground belonging to the old School, but there
was a piece of ground beyond the Churchyard sometimes used by the
boys.'

In 1749 on the new site on the edge of town the Manor House had
'two or more closes thereto adjoining ... One of these was converted
into a playground ... From time to time additions have been made to

21. The Five Chimneys, Tothill Fields, now Vincent Square. 'A favourite place of resort for Westminster boys in the eighteenth and early nineteenth centuries, especially for the hire of guns for shooting snipe, and skates for winter sports.' John Field (1987), *The King's Nurseries*

this playground by the throwing into it of adjoining enclosures – to form the present School Close' for cricket and football. (Book of Rugby School 1856.) Like Winchester and Eton, Rugby developed its own game of fives, making use of convenient walls to hit against.

Charterhouse was the last of the old Public Schools to be founded (1611), and was a boarding school from the start. There was a grassed area, 'The Green', which was uneven and by the early 19th century was 'full of holes and quite unfit for the playing of games'. It was 'gravelled, and thus we played cricket in the stones'.[10] Football too was played here, and there was a season for hoops.

After the Earl of Norfolk came into possession of the old Charterhouse monastery, he built in 1571 a cloister, or more properly a covered passage to link his new house to his tennis court. The latter became home to the Gownboys (scholars), and the cloister provided space on wet days for a form of very violent football, as well as for its own season of hoops.

At another London school, Christ's Hospital there was no grass surface, but Samuel Pepys, a governor of the school, complained in 1682 of the deplorable discipline of the scholars, 'even to the playing of football'.

The 18th century

With the great increase in the numbers of boarders throughout the century team games flourished at the public schools. The writer Horace Walpole, no games enthusiast, who entered Eton in 1726 wrote: 'Playing at cricket, as well as thrashing bargemen, was common at that time there.' In later years he would not risk a journey through the Abbey cloisters even to visit his mother's grave, because Westminster boys played football there. Of Warren Hastings, who left Westminster in 1749, it is related that 'few could beat him with a pair of sculls'. His contemporary at Westminster, the poet William Cowper, in a letter recalls: 'When I was a boy I excelled at cricket and football, but the fame I acquired by achievements in that way is long since forgotten, and I do not know that I have made a figure in anything since.' Cricket and football are two in a long list of games played at Eton in 1766, along with Fives, Battledores, Hopscotch, Hoops, Marbles, Trap-ball, Kites, Humming Tops, Hunt the Hare, and a score of less readily identifiable games. Beau Brummell who was in the Eleven of 1793 distinguished himself at Eton as the best scholar, the best boatman, and the best cricketer. At Charterhouse the song first sung in 1794 contains the stirring lines:

> I challenge all the men alive
> To say they e'er were gladder
> Than boys all striving who should kick
> Most wind out of the bladder.

It maybe assumed that football, at the end of the century, was a game played exclusively by boys.

Hoops

Hoops is included in the list of games played at Eton in 1766, and it was also popular elsewhere. The future Prime Minister, Lord John Russell, while a boy at the school 'carefully noted in the Diary which he kept at Westminster under the date October 4th 1803 "hoop and peashooters are out of fashion and football's come in".'

Hoops was a game for individuals, but sometimes a competitive one. Like other games such as Diabolo, Yo-yo, Skateboard and Frisbee, appearing in different decades of the 20th century, as well as the perennial Conkers and Kites, Hoops depended on a simple but ingenious piece of equipment; and since it demanded much practice and no little skill, it provided a challenge to young boys in particular. Hoops had its short annual season, but it possessed far more staying power over the years than the more modern passing crazes.

A Colleger who came to Eton in 1799 at the age of 8 refers to 'a little skirmishing with some Oppidans at hoops, a favourite and healthy sport in the autumn and winter season, in the schoolyard and cloisters; and in the exercise of which some pretty hard blows arise; and when opposed to each other, which is always the case, the Colleger, rather presumptuously, considers himself equal to at least three Oppidans, something like John Bull's estimate of his opposite neighbour's fighting qualities'. [11] Even in the second decade of the 19th century the October half was 'hoop time' for all boys below the Fifth Form.

Hoops in this period must have been widespread. They can be seen in playground pictures of Rugby, Christ's Hospital, Harrow, Durham and elsewhere; but it is at Charterhouse that the game appears to have been most developed, and in a less confrontational style than at Eton.

> There was near Old Charterhouse a tavern called the Crown Inn, from which the Oxford coach used to start every morning. Now Carthusians at that period [1778] were great hands at playing with hoops, the great feat being able to drive four at once. With these fours-in-hand, they used to have races in imitation of the Oxford coach, the starting point being the boundary wall on the east side of Upper Green, on which Lord Ellenborough, then at Charterhouse, painted a Crown to represent the Crown Inn. [12]
>
> In 1821 ... hoop-racing was a better game than our modern pride might lead us to esteem it. To drive four big hoops at once round a square space of nearly a quarter of a mile with sharp angles on it ... must certainly have needed no small skill and have had some fine exercise about it. [13]
>
> Hoops came in for a fortnight at the beginning of the Oration quarter, and consisted in 'tooling', i.e. driving two hoops – to 'tool' a single one was low and contemptible – up and down Cloisters, and also round Green, but in this last sometimes three were used, and even four by great proficients. To 'tool' a pair of hoops up and down Cloisters in a crowd of other pairs similarly engaged was a performance of no little skill, and to turn at each end a matter of great nicety and neatness of handling ... Another play-ground peculiarity was that after the hoop season the hoops ... were 'stored' or 'skied' into the branching elms from which they were again brought down by hockey-sticks flung at them. [14]

Cricket

Cricket is first mentioned in the 16th century. By the 18th century it was the game that had made the greatest advance. (It was fortunate that it was also the game that was most respectable in the eyes of headmasters.) By the end of the 18th century it was well on its way to becoming the English national game, crossing the barriers of class.

« LE JEU DE LA CROSSE »
Par Gravelot, *Petit cahier d'images pour les enfants*.

22. All our court games derive from the French *jeu de paume* in one way or another. Our football *may* have been introduced from France. But Cricket? In the 18th century the curved stick was common to the hitting games – La Crosse, cricket, Irish hurling, shinty, hockey, golf. In 1789 the Duke of Dorset, Ambassador at the Court of Louis XVI, arranged for the Earl of Tankerville to bring over a team of cricketers to France to play an exhibition match. They were met at Dover by the Duke whom the outbreak of Revolution had forced to return to England. Both Duke and Earl were fine cricketers, active members of the M.C.C. and patrons of the game. Cricket being a game full of subtlety and skill, similar in these respects to La Paume (tennis), it might have appealed to the French Court with who knows what results had not fate intervened; but France at the Revolution forfeited its leading position as social arbiter and purveyor of games.

23. Cricket in 1743, engraved by B. Cole

Of Publick Cricket Matches

Would it not be extremely odd to see Lords and Gentlemen, Clergymen and Lawyers, associating themselves with Butchers and Coblers in Pursuit of their Diversions? Or can there be Anything more absurd than making such Matches, for the sake of Profit, which is to be shared amongst People so remote in their Quality and Circumstances? Cricket is certainly a very innocent, and wholesome Exercise; yet it may be abused, if either great or little People make it their Business. It is greatly abused when it is made the Subject of publick Advertisements to draw together great Crowds of People, who ought all of them to be somewhere else. Noblemen, Gentlemen and Clergymen, have certainly a Right to divert themselves in what Manner they think fit; nor do I dispute their Privilege of making Butchers, Coblers or Tinkers their Companions, provided these are qualified to keep them Company. But I very much doubt whether they have any Right to invite Thousands of People to be Spectators of their Agility, at the Expence of their Duty and Honesty. The Time of People of Fashion may be indeed of very little Value, but, in a trading Country, the Time of the meanest Man ought to be of some Worth to himself, and to the Community. *British Champion* (1743)

Most of the best cricketers were professionals (Players), but all the leading amateurs (Gentlemen) were members of the Marylebone Club at old Lord's which in 1788 issued the first effective Laws of Cricket and which was acknowledged as the supreme authority on the game. Almost the first match of which details are preserved was played in 1746 between Old Westminsters and Old Etonians; and in

24. 'New Articles of the Game of Cricket, 1785. As revised and settled at the Star and Garter, Pall Mall, February 25th 1774 by the Committee of Noblemen & Gentlemen of Kent etc.' They became members of the Marylebone Club, which published the first authoritative rules in 1788. The middle stump was introduced in 1777.

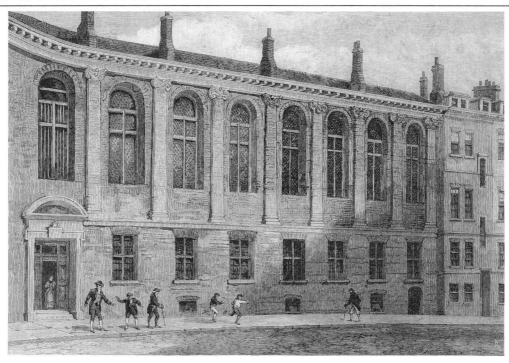

25. Merchant Taylors' School was founded in 1561 by the Worshipful Company of Merchant Taylors. (The original building was burnt down in 1666 and was rebuilt in 1675.) For three centuries it remained in Suffolk Lane, Cannon Street (see above). In 1875 it was moved to Charterhouse Square, whence Charterhouse had moved to Godalming in 1872. In 1933 it was again moved, to Sandy Lodge, Northwood, Middlesex.

'The Game of Cricket. An Exercise at Merchant Taylors' School' by Samuel Bishop (boy, 3rd Undermaster, and from 1783 Headmaster of Merchant Taylors' School). *The Gentleman's Magazine Vol. XXVI* (October 1756)

Peace, and her arts, we sing – her genial pow'r
Can give the breast to pant, the tho't to low'r,
Tho' guiltless, not inglorious souls inspires,
And boasts less savage, not less noble fires.
Such is her sway, when Cricket calls her train,
The sons of labour, to the accustom'd plain,
With all the hero's passion and desire,
They swell, they glow, they envy, and admire:
Despair and resolution reign by turns;
Suspense torments, and emulation burns.
See! in due rank dispos'd, intent they stand,
In act to start – the eye, the foot, the hand,
Still active, eager, seem conjoin'd in one;
Tho' fixt, all moving, and while present gone.
In ancient combat, from the Parthian steed,
Not more unerring flew the barbed reed
Than rolls the ball, with vary'd vigour play'd,
Now levell'd, whizzing o'er the springing blade,
Now toss'd to rise more fatal from the ground,
Exact and faithful to th' appointed bound,
Yet vain its speed, yet vain its certain aim;
The wary batsman watches o'er the game:
Before his stroke the leathern circle flies,
Now wheels oblique, now mounting threats the skies.
Nor yet less vain the wary batsman's blow,

If intercepted by the circling foe,
Too soon the nimble arm retorts the ball,
Or ready fingers catch it in its fall:
Thus various art with vary'd fortune strives,
And with each changing chance the sport revives.
Emblem of many colour'd life – the state
By Cricket-rules discriminates the great:
The outward side, who place and profit want,
Watch to surprize, and labour to supplant:
While those who taste the sweets of present winnings,
Labour as heartily to keep their innings,
On either side the whole great game is play'd,
Untry'd no shift is left, unsought no aid:
Skill vies with skill, & pow'r contends with pow'r,
And squint ey'd prejudice computes the score.
In private life, like single handed play'rs,
We get less notches, but we meet less cares.
Full many a lusty effort, which at court
Would fix the doubtful issue of the sport,
Wide of its mark, or impotent to rise,
Ruins the rash, and disappoints the wise.
Yet all in public, and in private, strive
To keep the ball of action still alive,
And just to all, when each his ground has run,
Death tips the wicket, and the game is done.

1751 the Gentlemen of England met Eton College Past and Present at Newmarket in a series of three matches for a £1500 stake, won by the Gentlemen.

While boys were playing team games with enthusiasm there is no record of a match between schools until the last decades of the century. The first recorded inter-school cricket match was played in 1786. The bare details are contained in the Spencer-Stanhope MSS in the Westminster School Archives:

Westminster against Eton Friday May ye 26 1786

		E	
W 1st Innings	149	88	61 to tye ye W. score
2nd Innings	94	155	two wickets to go down
	243	243	

Was it a draw, in Eton's favour, as it would be to-day? Was it a tie? Was it a win for Westminster, based on 1st Innings result? In any case, an exciting game for the first inter-school match, whether officially sanctioned or not.

The second known school cricket match, again between Eton and Westminster, took place in 1796 on Hounslow Heath. The Hon. Edward Harbord wrote to his father, Lord Suffield:

> The Westminster boys are going to play us at cricket; we meet at Hounslow, and there is to be determined the fate of Eton! or I think rather of Westminster. The Masters know nothing about it, nor are they intended to do so, I believe, till it is over. So I suppose the Eton boys when they come back will be rewarded with a comfortable, reasonable and proper present of birch, together with a few thousand lines of some book to translate or to say by heart, or whatever pleases Dr Heath, which most certainly the heroic eleven will submit to, supposing that they return conquerors. I think the Etonians can now overcome the Westminster boys in anything.

He guessed right about the present of birch – Dr Heath flogged them all the next morning, a future Prime Minister, Lord Melbourne, among them; but they did not return conquerors. Westminster won by 66 runs.

Early 19th century

In the difficult early years of the 19th century the headmaster of a public school could do little more than the master of a grammar school to supervise time outside the schoolroom. Although the late 18th-century enclosures probably restricted their ability to swarm over the countryside, boys, raised on the country sports of their forefathers, still invaded the neighbourhood, bird-nesting, fishing, duck-shooting, poaching and raiding chicken-runs. With so few assistant masters effective control was difficult. In any case at this time their role was not seen as extending beyond the schoolroom. At Eton in 1829 there were 8 masters for 556 boys in the Upper School. A headmaster could only maintain discipline by fear and frequent floggings. As cricket, football and boating became more popular free-time alternatives to field-sports, games organised, it must be emphasised, entirely by boys, headmasters could appreciate that they had been presented with a way of controlling and expending the surplus energy of a large number of boys. Matches with other schools were an altogether different proposition. To give leave to boys to travel to another school on their own was asking for trouble, and where the venue was a public place the risk was greater still ...

In 1799, three years after the illicit match on Hounslow Heath, the Eton and Westminster XIs were allowed to meet at Thomas Lord's first ground in what is now Dorset Square off Baker Street, and again in 1800 and 1801. Westminster lost easily on the last two occasions (in 1801 no one reaching double figures), and there is no record of further matches. In 1805 (the year of Trafalgar) during the holidays at Lord's Eton beat Harrow by an innings and 2 runs. Lord Byron played for Harrow, in fact he is said to have had a part in arranging

26. View of Harrow, 1802.

the match. According to Arthur Shakespeare, a member of the Harrow XI, 'Lord Byron insisted on playing and was allowed a person to run for him, his lameness impeding him so much.' Eton had a poet of her own:

> Adventurous boys of Harrow School
> Of cricket you've no knowledge.
> Ye played not cricket but the fool
> With men of Eton College.

Byron's neat riposte:

> Ye Eton wits to play the fool
> Is not the boast of Harrow School.
> No wonder then at our defeat –
> Folly like yours could ne'er be beat.

Byron wrote to a friend:

> We have played the Eton and were most confoundedly beat; however it was some comfort to me that I got 11 notches the lst Innings and 7 the 2d ... After the match we dined together, and were extremely friendly, not a single discordant note was uttered by either party. To be sure, we were most of us rather drunk,and went together to the Haymarket Theatre, where we kicked up a row, as you may suppose, when so many Harrovians and Etonians meet at one place. I was one of seven in a single hackney, 4 Eton and 3 Harrow, and then we all got into the same box.

The scorebook records just half the claimed number of Byronic notches. Dr Charles Merivale, Dean of Ely (1818-24) recalls 'The remark was once made to me by Mr John Arthur Lloyd ... who had been captain of the School [and also of the Eleven], "Yes", he said, "Byron played in that match, and very badly too. He should never have been in the eleven if my counsel had been taken".' [Lloyd himself took wickets, but earned a pair of spectacles.] (Percy M. Thornton 1885)*, Harrow School and Its Surroundings*

Played at Old Lord's Ground, August 2, 1805

Harrow

Lord Ipswich	b Carter	10	b Heaton	21
T. Farrer	b Carter	7	c Bradley	3
T. Dury	b Carter	0	st Heaton	6
– Bolton	run out	2	b Heaton	0
*J. A. Lloyd	b Carter	0	b Carter	0
A. Shakespeare	st Heaton	8	run out	5
Lord Byron	c Barnard	7	b Carter	2
Hon. T. Erskine	b Carter	4	b Heaton	8

W. Brockman	b Heaton	9	b Heaton		10
E. Stanley	not out	3	c Canning		7
T. Asheton	b Carter	3	not out		0
	B	2	B		3
		55			65

Eton

W. B. Heaton	b Lloyd	0
– Slingsby	b Shakespeare	29
T. Carter	b Shakespeare	3
– Farhill	c Lloyd	6
S. Canning	c Farrer	12
– Camplin	b Ipswich	42
– Bradley	b Lloyd	16
– Barnard	b Shakespeare	0
– Barnard	not out	3
J. Kaye	b Lord Byron	7
H. Dover	c Bolton	4
		122

Eton won by an innings and 2 runs.

Catches and stumpings were not yet universally credited to the bowler. Bowling was under-arm, with the hand lower than the elbow at delivery. Round-arm, with hand lower than the shoulder, was legalised in 1835, and over-arm, with hand higher than the shoulder, was eventually recognised in 1864.

This was the first match between Eton and Harrow the score of which is preserved, although there are said to have been a few others previously. 'The next recorded match is 1818, but several are known to have taken place between these periods.' [15] In 1822 began the series of annual matches at Mr Lord's third and final ground at St John's Wood, the oldest continuous fixture in the cricket calendar. It was played at the start of the holidays. The year before the captains had arranged a match at Eton, but at the last moment Dr Keate (1809-34), who had himself opened for Eton in 1791, banned it. Harrow won by 88, 'besides running 15 short notches ... As the Collegers [at Eton] were not allowed, owing to the expense, to become members of the Boats, and the Oppidans had no regular cricket ground owing to College's first claim on the scanty playing fields, the majority of the XI were habitually Collegers. There were seven in the 1836 Eleven.' [16] Collegers were first admitted to the Eight in 1864, and to the Field Eleven in 1866.

It was the brothers Christopher and Charles Wordsworth (nephews of the poet), when captains respectively of Winchester and Harrow, who arranged their first match, at Lord's on 27 and 28 July

27. Mr Lord's third cricket ground, before the fire destroyed the original pavilion in 1825.

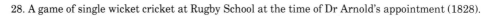

28. A game of single wicket cricket at Rugby School at the time of Dr Arnold's appointment (1828).

1825. They were later to exchange allegiances, Christopher becoming Headmaster of Harrow and Charles Second Master of Winchester. Winchester won by 135. In the early hours of the next morning the one-room pavilion was destroyed by fire, with the sad loss of early cricket records and scorebooks. Next year, 1826, in this now triangular festival week Winchester beat both Eton and Harrow. Against Harrow W. Meyrick scored 146 not out, the first recorded inter-school century. Harrow were skittled for 29 in their first innings and Winchester won by 382. The *Annals of Sporting and Fancy Gazette* records: 'The Wintonians were giants, the others pigmies in the comparison.' The stature of the former was enhanced by the 'high white, or rather yellowish, beaver hats' worn by the Eleven at Lord's. We wore a pink silk jersey a survival no doubt of the old archery days and a high top hat.' [17]

The Shrewsbury Hunt

At Shrewsbury Samuel Butler allowed cricket, but, he denounced Shrewsbury's brand of football (dowling) as 'fit only for butcher boys ... more fit for farm boys and labourers than young gentlemen'; and he threatened the Severn watermen he would have them up before the magistrates if they hired out boats to Shrewsbury boys. Towards The Royal Shrewsbury School Hunt he was more tolerant.

> For many years past one of the most popular institutions at Shrewsbury School has been the R.S.S.H. or Royal Shrewsbury School Hunt. It is of course the old school game of 'Hare and Hounds'; and although it can never have furnished the special excitements which belonged to the form of the game known at Eton and Harrow as 'Jack O'Lantern' [A Run at night, the hare carrying a light.], the R.S.S.H. is noteworthy for its elaborate constitution, under which each boy finds his place, either as huntsman, whip, gentleman, or hound. (It should be noted in connection with the independent origin of the game at Shrewsbury that the two boys who carry scent have always been called foxes and never hares.) For many years too the delights of the runs were intensified by the fact that they were carried on in complete contempt of all

29. The Royal Shrewsbury School Hunt, 'Dr Butler's Hounds Killing', 1834.

30. The Huntsman, 1834.

school regulations as to bounds; and their popularity was further increased by the perpetual feuds which they caused with the neighbouring farmers. (On one occasion a complaint as to the hounds 'trespassing' led first to a general punishment, then to broken windows, and lastly to the whole school being sent home a week before the holidays.) ... The history of the R.S.S.H. has been regularly recoreded in the run books from the year 1842, but the institution is of much earlier origin. Old Salopians are still living who remember the runs in Dr Butler's days [1798-1836], and relate with pride their attainment of the honour of being pronounced killing hound or killing gentleman. These honours were gained, then as now, by the hound or gentleman who 'killed'; that is to say, who came in first in a race at the finish the greatest number of times during the season. Dr Butler does not appear to have interfered with the runs ... and they met with no hindrance in the early years of Dr Kennedy's head-mastership. For a long time Dr Kennedy does not appear to have been aware of the extent to which the runs were carried on 'out of bounds' ... His eyes, however, were opened ... in 1843 or 1844 by the disappearance of a large number of copies of the new Latin Grammar, (The first edition of Dr Kennedy's Elementary Latin Grammar was published in 1843), which had taken the form of scent, and a temporary check on the operations of the hounds ensued ... Up to 1856, though tolerated by the Head Master, they had never received his sanction. In that year ... having first threatened to put a stop to the runs altogether by multiplying 'callings over', he offered to sanction them ... on condition that the praepostors pledged themselves in writing that they should be carried on under certain fixed regulations ... The use of the paper scent, which from the precision with which the line of country to be taken in each particular run is now arranged, is no longer necessary. George W. Fisher (1899), *Annals of Shrewsbury School*

Opposition came from farmers who attacked the runners with sticks and set bloodhounds on them, and this is not surprising when one reads that 'the first two gates offered no resistance, being utterly smashed by the running multitude', and that 'fencing' – that is to say breaking down hedges – was a recognised part of the game. Equally natural was the opposition of the School authorities, as a letter of L.W. Denman (1834-9) tells how, after a run, the members of the Hunt used to go to the Dog and Partridge Inn 'to take a glass of ale and smoke a pipe', while stops for sherry and other drinks in the middle of a run were common, and on one occasion they were provided at a farm 'two magnificent bowls of punch and as much beer as we could drink' – after which the run was continued. J. Basil Oldham (1952), *A History of Shrewsbury School*

Dr Kennedy (1836-66), Butler's pupil and successor, was more positive in his attitude to games than his predecessor. In a letter to the Bishop of Lichfield he wrote that boys should have 'the means of innocent amusement and exercise in their leisure hours', and he saw the advantage of games as an antidote to poaching and lawlessness.He provided a field for them, and from 1837 allowed boating on the Severn. Shrewsbury's first school match on the water was in 1864 against Cheltenham. It was rowed in Fours at Shrewsbury, and

Cheltenham won by three seconds. An annual match continued until 1894.

Boating

Although there had been boating on the Thames at Eton openly for many years, it was not officially recognised or permitted. It was regarded by successive headmasters as a disreputable sport. The river was dangerous for non-swimmers, and was in use as a common sewer; it was also busy with barge traffic and the haunt of rough characters. Only in 1840 was boating officially recognised at Eton, by which time the Eton VIII had rowed against Westminster four times on the Thames in eagerly awaited and fully reported races.

Football

At a time when football games were everywhere dead or dying, fate supplied place, players and opportunity for its rebirth through the public schools. In the first half of the 19th century, when school bounds were enforced and a playing-field was provided, large numbers of boys, possessed of the excess energy and competitive spirit of youth as well as the natural affinity of boys for a ball, took advantage of their extensive leisure hours to organise daily games of football during the winter months. It would have been surprising had each school not developed its own game and eventually written its own code of rules, refined over the years. Nowhere else at the time did such privileged and ideal circumstances present themselves. All these games involved handling to a greater or lesser degree. Before 'kicking' the ball with the head was introduced in the 1870s, the natural way of dealing with a bounding ball was either to stop it with the hand or to catch it, take three or four paces and kick, just as that anomaly the Association goalkeeper does to-day. At Eton three games had evolved, each with its own rules to suit the different playground features. Two of them 'At the Wall' and 'In the Field' survive. (The third 'Lower College', with goals marked on trees, was discontinued in 1865.)

There were distinct games at Westminster and at Charterhouse too; just as there necessarily are today at all schools where playground or sportshall football takes place. Winchester, Eton and Harrow still remain loyal to their own individual and excellent games, with rules refined over the years.

They are especially interesting in being survivals from an earlier age of football. In Harrow's 'Footer' and Eton's Field Game can be seen elements of the old upright scrum, strict offside game. Winchester Football, on its narrow 27 x 80 yards 'canvas' and with its emphasis on low kicking, must relate to some circumscribed former playground where the kickers were inhibited by the differing restraints, either of buildings, or hilltop, or boundary of lordly cricket

31. A 'Hot' at Foot Ball, Winchester. Twenty-two and Twenty-two in the 1830s. 'The matches between College and Commoners were not played on Canvas at all, but … along Meads Wall with no boundary except that made by the legs of College and Commoner onlookers.'

ground. Dowling survived at Shrewsbury until 1903. Fags were called douls (dowls) from the Greek doulos, a slave, and dowling was fagging. As at Rugby, Winchester, Harrow and elsewhere, the little boys had to fag at the game by defending the goal, or by lining the touch-line to keep the ball in play.[18]

Shrewsbury, Eton, Winchester and Harrow all later embraced the Association code as an additional game, Harrow changing to Rugby Union in 1927. The Charterhouse and Westminster games, though different, were particularly important, as with their practice of limited off-side they provided the distinguishing feature of Association Football. From 1863 the two schools have played an annual match. At Rugby the daring tactic of running with the ball was initiated in the 1820s, becoming more popular in the late 1830s, when it aroused enthusiastic shouts of 'Hack him down'. It was legalised in 1841-2, and the game eventually developed into Rugby Union; but Rugby with its huge number of players and its unique Big Side dimensions and hazards did not welcome another school at football until Cheltenham won in 1896.[19] By then trees and other obstacles had been removed, and the next year the Captain of Football cut down the ground to Rugby Union dimensions. The first inter-school football match in England played to Rugby School rules (more or less) was Marlborough v. Clifton (20-a-side) in 1864, when differing interpretations of the rules almost led to its abandonment and discouraged further 'foreign' contests. (The two schools next met twenty-seven years later in 1891.) When a school issued a challenge it was not always accepted.

> A challenge was also sent by the Charterhouse to play them at cricket, which was very properly refused, not only on account of their being inferior players, but because it was thought beneath Westminster to accept a challenge from a private school. *The Westminster Cricket Ledger* (1818)

In the 1840s St Paul's and King's College School also received rebuffs from Westminster; and in 1866 the message was the same.

> Sir,
> The Captain of the Westminster Eleven is sorry to disappoint Shrewsbury, but Westminster plays no schools except public schools, and the general feeling in the school quite coincides with that of the Committee of the Public Schools Club who issue this list of public schools – Charterhouse, Eton, Harrow, Rugby, Westminster and Winchester.
>
> Yours truly
> E. Oliver, Captain.

32. Charterhouse, 1805. Still only two stumps. The Cloisters in the background.

Sir,

I cannot allow your answer to my first letter to pass without some notice. I have only to say that a school, which we have Camden's authority for stating was the most important school in England [schola totius Angliae numerosissima] at a time when Westminster was unknown, which Her Majesty has included in the list of public schools by the Royal Commission, and which, according to the report of the Commissioners, is more distinctly public than any other school, cannot be deprived of its rank as a public school either by the insolent assertions of a Westminster boy, or by the dictum of the self-styled Public Schools Club. I regret to find from your letter that the Captain of the Westminster Eleven has yet to learn the first lesson of a true public school education, the behaviour due from one gentleman to another.

I am, Sir,
Your obedient servant
J. Spencer Phillips, Captain.[20]

Ironically, when William Camden first published his Britannia in 1586, he was Usher at Westminster and later became its Headmaster.

The Victorian Public Schools

Numbers at most of the public schools were high at the start of the 19th century, but the late 1820s, the 1830s and 1840s were a bad period for nearly all of them. A reaction had set in against their obvious defects – the barbaric living conditions, the narrow syllabus, the neglect of religion, and the gross indiscipline. These flaws were first highlighted by the frequent rebellions, inspired by the French Revolution, which broke out in all the schools in the last years of the 18th and the first quarter of the 19th century, when headmasters tried to wrest back the privileges surrendered to the senior boys, whose rule over their juniors was absolute. (At Eton in 1820 all 280 VIth and Vth formers could fag the 248 lower boys.) Apart from Arnold's Rugby, and Eton which continued to thrive despite virulent attacks in the Whig press, all other public schools lost pupils in significant numbers, Westminster, Harrow and Charterhouse each dropping below one hundred at one stage during the 1830s or 1840s; and even Rugby and Eton had temporary losses.

But the beginning of the Victorian era proved to be a new dawning. The Industrial Revolution had brought about a great increase in and a spreading of wealth. It had also created a widening demand for education, especially boarding education, by the newly enriched middle classes, who saw these schools as a way to social advancement. The railways which the Industrial Revolution had spawned had revolutionised travel, so that long distance journeys to school were now practicable and very much cheaper than by coach. The old public schools benefitted from this, but there were wider effects. The Elizabethan Age had seen the foundation or re-founding of a great number of grammar schools, many endowed by rich merchants (as were Rugby and Harrow) ending in 1619 with Dulwich. After more than two centuries of stagnation the Victorian Age was to experience a similar wave of foundations of boarding rather than day schools, heralded by Cheltenham in 1841: Marlborough, Rossall, Brighton, Radley, Taunton, Lancing and Hurstpierpoint in the 1840s; Bradfield, St John's (Leatherhead), Wellington, Epsom and Ardingly in the 1850s; Bloxham, Clifton, Haileybury, Malvern, Cranleigh, St Edward's, Eastbourne, Denstone and Monkton Combe in the 1860s, among others. Most of these schools were founded by groups of men interested in education (the Proprietors) who appointed the headmaster, and they were known as Proprietary Schools. This distinguished them from Private Schools where the headmaster was also the proprietor. Rugby was the model, rather than Eton; and there was a strong evangelising inspiration behind the foundation of very many of them, notably the group of schools founded by the Rev. Nathaniel Woodard.

For the old endowed grammar schools too the new climate offered opportunities. In 1797 the Governors of Leeds Grammar School (1552) had attempted through the Court of Chancery to amend their statutes which limited instruction to Latin and Greek, in order that more practical subjects such as arithmetic and a modern language could be taught, so as to benefit the citizens of a growing commercial city. Judgement was eventually given in 1805 by the Lord Chancellor, Lord Eldon. The intention of the founder was what counted, not 'the benefit of the Merchants of Leeds', and the limiting statute was binding. In 1840 pressure for change brought an Act of Parliament which gave the Court of Chancery the power to amend the statutes of a school, and in 1869 the Endowed Schools Act was passed. The year before, the Public Schools Act had altered the statutes of the Clarendon seven. The new Act, which followed another Royal Commission Report, had the same effect on the rest of the secondary schools. It empowered three Commissioners to approve new statutes for 782 grammar schools and over 100 proprietary and private schools, and also to apply the endowments of obsolete grammar schools and chantries for educational purposes. A number of schools, with the help of the Court of Chancery, had already seized the opportunity to become public boarding schools – those that had the space and sufficient endowments to expand and, above all, a headmaster with the vision and ability to succeed, like Thring of Uppingham. So too, in course of time, Abingdon, Aldenham, Giggleswick, Oundle, Repton, Sedbergh, Sherborne, St Bees, St Peter's (York), Tonbridge and many others. Some schools, like Abingdon (1563), could only expand by moving out of their cramped town-centre schoolroom to a new site on the outskirts.

Tonbridge	1843	43	1875	235
Sherborne	1850	40	1877	278
Uppingham	1853	25	1887	320
Repton	1854	50	1874	250

(Some examples of increased numbers)

Another aspect of this movement was provided by the Court of Chancery case brought by the people of Harrow against Harrow School for disregard of John Lyon's stated purpose to educate the 'poor boys of the parish'. The 1811 judgement found for the school: John Lyon's intention was that instruction should be confined to the classics, and parish boys would not benefit from studying them exclusively. Following the Endowed Schools Act of 1869 restitution was made to the people of Harrow when, with the funds made available, the Lower School of John Lyon was established as a local day school in 1876. The Lower School of Lawrence Sheriff at Rugby, Alleyn's School at Dulwich, Judd and Skinners' schools at Tonbridge and Tunbridge Wells are other examples of a founder's charitable intentions being belatedly respected.[21]

'Manly and Muscular Diversions'

The 1830s and 1840s, when numbers at most of the public schools were low, saw the final acceptance of team games by headmasters, not yet as part of the curriculum, but as voluntary free-time activities. Dr Arnold at Rugby (1828-42), the most influential headmaster of his or any other day, did not think games were important educationally, but he tolerated them and even appeared on the touchline. The many Rugby masters who went on to be headmasters of other schools took with them the educational ideas of Arnold and his ideal of the Christian gentleman.[22] They had a dedicated enthusiasm for what they had experienced at Rugby, including its version of football. Without these men (and Tom Brown) it is questionable whether Rugby Football would have expanded any further than have Winchester, Eton or Harrow Football.

One of them, George Cotton (1851-8) (Tom Brown's 'young master'), arrived at Marlborough from Rugby in 1851, a few months after the last serious public school rebellion. Marlborough had started in 1843 with 200 boys, most of them from country vicarages, (but with no playing fields). They quickly got out of hand and roamed the countryside, poaching, and provoking local farmers. Cotton's predecessor had applied unpopular 'private school' supervision, which incited the rebellion. Cotton, following Arnold's bold example, entrusted senior boys with authority; and he introduced organised games, putting youthful energies to better purpose. Marlborough's contribution to the development of Rugby Union was to prove hardly less important than Rugby's.

The increased number of boarding-schools helped the development of games, and encouraged competition between them. The acceptance of organised sport as an important part of school life was now shared by headmasters of old and new establishments alike. Dr Vaughan (1845-59), who in his youth had hated games, said:

At Harrow it is thought almost discreditable not to play, and play well, at some game. And I am happy to say that very many, if not almost all, of our successful scholars have been great also in the school games.

At Winchester Dr Moberly (1835-66) had said: 'The idle boys. I mean the boys who play cricket', but his successor Dr Ridding (1866-84) was to claim: 'Give me a boy who is a cricketer. I can make something of him'.

Radley was founded in 1847, and the first Warden and co-founder, the Rev. Robert Singleton (1847-51), confides to his diary in June 1848:

> The boys are bent upon having a band among themselves ... I had them up to my room [now Common Room] today and spoke at some length on the importance of what they were about ... not in a musical point of view (tho' I did not want to under-rate that), but in a moral. Their education was by no means confined to the School-room, but a serious part of it was carried on in their play-hours; a healthy play was equally necessary with close study to the advance of virtue. The great thing was to be always employed; the devil hated industry. That in this view alone the cultivation of skill on a musical instrument was of consequence provided it did not interfere with cricket, and other manly and muscular diversions [He went on to say:] But besides, as a far higher consideration, the practice which it would require had a manifest tendency to promote patience, industry, and other good habits, which it was in no small degree the object in studying Latin and Greek to infuse.

Singleton's enthusiasm for football was such that he wrote a football song. (Chorus: 'For There is Not a Game Of all Those I Could Name to Compare with the Merry Football'.) James Baker, a Fellow (Master) under Singleton, in a letter to his father in October 1849 wrote:

> With regard to the question about games, I wish Mr Leigh could have seen a game of football that was played in the Park to-day, about 30 on a side; though they have not yet arrived at a very precise code of laws on the subject, yet one is gradually growing up, especially among the little boys who generally have a distinct game of their own and certainly a very spirited one ... Cricket is certainly encouraged by us as much as possible ... Fives flourishes very much, specially the Winchester Bat Fives, or at least something like it with Bats from Winchester.

Singleton and his co-founder, and third Warden, the Rev. William Sewell (1853-61) had been involved in the founding (1843) of St Columba's in Ireland, Sewell as one of the four founders and Singleton as Warden. In his Journal of Residence at St Columba's Sewell notes in 1844: 'Glad to see the Fellows playing football with the boys, and cricket.' The boys had two Fours on the Boyne, and Sewell wrote a Latin boating-song for them. At Radley, well on in his fifties, he was proud of his prowess on the fives court against First Form boys.

Radley's first school cricket match was in 1853, a home defeat by Bradfield: 53 in reply to 99. Bradfield's top scorer was 25 Radley

33. Radley, 1859. Cricket in 'College caps' (mortar-boards).

wides.[23] Radley's first school football match was at Bradfield in 1864. Played to the home side's rules, based on Winchester Football, it was 'tied' 1-1. The fixture was temporarily dropped next year. 'It had roused considerable feeling in the previous year, and this, we believe, was the reason for its abandonment'.[24] Bradfield went over to 'soccer' in 1869, and Radley followed suit in 1881, changing to 'rugger' in 1914.

In the same year that Sewell became Warden of Radley the Rev. Edward Thring started his long and distinguished headmastership of Uppingham (1853-87). He too played fives in his fifties, as well as earlier appearing on the cricket and football fields. He writes in his diary: 'I could not help thinking with some pride what headmaster of a great school had ever played at football before. Would either dignity or shins suffer for it? I doubt it.' There was at least one other

34. Cricket at Bradfield, 1865.

headmaster who played football occasionally. This was Dr John Collis of Bromsgrove (1843-67), a Rugbeian.

> He was a plump man and was fond of catching the ball on the bounce. But he never ran. He stood stock still with the ball in his arms, and the players swarmed round him like bees. In due course things became serious for Dr Collis and cries would be heard from the centre of the scrimmage – till the Doctor dropped the ball.[25]

By the mid-19th century, with the support of headmasters, cricket, football, fives, as well as boating where there was water, were an integral part of public school life.

Chapter 3

Fives

Died at his house in Burbage-street, St Giles's, John Cavanagh, the
famous hand fives-player. When a person dies, who does anything
better than any one else in the world, which so many others are trying
to do well, it leaves a gap in society. It is not likely that any one will
now see the game of fives played in its perfection for many years to
come – for Cavanagh is dead, and has not left his peer behind him. It
may be said that there are things of more importance than striking a
ball against a wall – there are things indeed which make more noise
and do as little good, such as making war and peace, making speeches
and answering them, making verses and blotting them; making money
and throwing it away. But the game of fives is what no one despises
who has ever played at it. It is the finest exercise for the body, and the
best relaxation for the mind ... He who takes to playing at fives is twice
young. He feels neither the past nor future 'in the instant'. Debts,
taxes, 'domestic treason, foreign levy, nothing can touch him further'.
He has no other wish, no other thought, from the moment the game
begins, but that of striking the ball, of placing it, of *making* it! This
Cavanagh was sure to do.... Sometimes, when he seemed preparing to
send the ball with the full swing of his arm, he would by a slight turn
of his wrist drop it within an inch of the line. In general, the ball came
from his hand, as if from a racket, in a straight horizontal line ... The
only peculiarity of his play was that he never *volleyed*, but let the balls
hop; but if they rose an inch from the ground, he never missed having
them. His service was tremendous. He once played Woodward and
Meredith together (two of the best players in England) ... and made
seven and twenty aces following by services alone – a thing unheard of
... Cavanagh was an Irishman by birth, and a house-painter by profes-
sion ... William Hazlitt (1819), *The Indian Jugglers*

The ancient game of handball is a natural one, wherever there is a
wall to hit a ball against. With hand or glove or other hand attach-
ment it is played all over the world. In *Handball Games of the World*
John Lolkama lists 45 varieties. It is popular in the U.S.A. and
handball is one of Ireland's national games. In England handball is
called Fives. The word Fives is of uncertain origin. The most obvious
reference is to the five fingers of the hand, as in 'a bunch of fives' for
the closed fist. Another possibility is as a game for five players. In
Rackets, Squash Rackets, Tennis, Fives and Badminton John Armitage writes of the word Fives: 'Once it could be applied to all games
played with the hand and the ball. And all games now played with a
racket were once played with the hand and known to everyone as
"Fives" ... Hand-ball across a net became Tennis [another word of

uncertain origin] in England. Yet for long afterwards it was frequently referred to as Fives, as also was the game of Rackets.'

Similarly, in France the ancient game of La Paume (palm), which is our (Real or Royal) Tennis, is played with a racket, but still retains its original name of La Paume. Paume (Tennis) was the only popular court game in France, as in England, from the Middle Ages to the end of the 18th century; but handball games could also be played in the covered courts against a wall or the angle of walls.

Winchester

In England the modern games called Fives, played against the walls of a court, were developed at the schools after which they are named; and because that is where the courts are, they are still largely confined to the public schools, their Old Boys, and the older universities. These are games started centuries ago when boys hit a ball against a convenient school wall where there was a solid enough floor to create a bounce. Sometimes hands, with or without gloves, sometimes wooden bats were used. At Winchester

> Ball Court ... dates from 1688. The glare of its chalk floor was trying both to fags and to the players of bat fives who were its legitimate occupants; concrete was first laid down (in the centre only) about 1851. The oldest court intended for hand-fives ... was built in 1862. *Winchester College 1393-1893*, 1893

Robert B. Mansfield, at Winchester from 1835-40, wrote:

> The bat used is, I believe, peculiar to Winchester; it was about two-and-a-half feet in length, the part with which the ball was struck expanding to about the size of a small lady's hand, and immediately above it the wood was planed thin, thus forming a powerful spring. With this instrument the ball could be driven with great force; and I have known it used for other purposes, for which it was very effectual, though not very agreeable to one of the parties in that game ... The balls used were small, about the size of a large grape-shot, and cost sixpence a piece, which made the game an expensive one; as if the ball passed to the right or to the left of the school wall against which we played, it vanished altogether from our ken ... The Winchester 'Bat Fives' was amusing enough when played in a promiscuous way, but not, I think, a really good game, as it was too difficult. I have scarcely ever seen even the best players return the ball more than three or four times. The Fags' share of the game was to stand round the edge of the Court and pick up the balls as they rolled off ... it was far from pleasant, owing to the blinding glare from the white concrete of which the floor was made. Robert B. Mansfield (1866), *School Life at Winchester College*

A little later, W.A. Fearon, a boy at Winchester 1852-9 and its Head Master from 1884-1901, remembers:

> Our beautiful game of Winchester bat fives. This was a game peculiar

to ourselves: it was difficult, but was most charming. It was played with a long narrow bat, very thin at the neck which gave it the spring, with a full thick knob at the point, where you hit the ball. If you caught the ball on the right point, the distance it sprang was magnificent; but woe betide you, if you caught it on the neck, your bat would infallibly be smashed. As interests multiplied such a special game couldn't last. I found it better to break up Ball Court, as its own proper game was dead. W.A. Fearon (1924), *Passing of Old Winchester*

The modern Winchester Fives court is rectangular, with a so-called 'buttress' (origin unknown), which in fact is a narrowing of the left-hand wall for two-thirds of its length from the back wall. The nine-and-three-quarter inch wide end of the buttress at an angle from the wall of 135 degrees is the only hazard, but a very important one.

35. A Winchester Fives Court.

Rugby

Fives has been played since before records were kept. [In 1839] the game was largely of a spontaneous character played in the Old Quadrangle where there was a ledge of convenient height all round the walls under the cloisters; and games in the porch leading in from High Street, which makes a particularly convenient, almost enclosed area, were a constant nuisance to peaceful passers-by. More formal games could be played in the assorted courts that stood against the north side of the rackets court ... These early courts varied in size and design, and one with no buttress was regarded as the best ... There was also a Bat Fives court, monopolised by the Upper School as it had been flagged at their expense, which had as its front wall the end of the School buildings next to the Birching Tower, and its back wall the side of a school built on to the vestry of the old Chapel; fags retrieved balls that went out of court on either side ... The demand for this court was such that another was built in 1848. When these courts made way for the New Quadrangle and Chapel, Thomson 'turner and fives-bat maker' was in the words of a letter to the Meteor 'saved from impending ruin' by [a master] who paid for the paving of a new court against the south wall of the old rackets court, but players could no longer enjoy the fun of throwing their broken bats on the School House roof.

Thomson's bats were made of a single flat piece of willow, some sixteen inches long, with an oval striking area, about the size of a man's hand, rather more than half an inch thick, reducing to only one-eighth of an inch as it narrowed towards the slim hand-carved handle: a very good twopence worth. The balls were leather-covered and hand-stitched; as they were only one inch in diameter, play on an unevenly floored court was impossible. J.B. Hope Simpson (1967), *Rugby Since Arnold*.

Although Rugby Fives was 'very popular' (in 1868) with pressure on courts for playing, 'in 1883 a writer in the Meteor could claim that "not above 20 fellows in the School play Fives", and in 1885 a Meteor editorial begins "Alas for Rugby Fives! To all appearances ... it is already at its last gasp". But by 1893 nearly 300 of the school's 450 were said to be players ... Bat Fives (see below) faded away in about

1904, and the Eton Fives Competition ended in 1913.' Eton Fives courts had been presented by two members of the staff in 1863

The Rugby Fives court to-day is a plain rectangle, with no buttress. Inter-school matches began in the 1870s and its laws were codified in 1930.

Westminster

Another game much played at all times and seasons was racquets, played either with what we called wire racquets – i.e. catgut – or with wooden racquets; these were made of, I think, ash wood, about six or six-and-a-half inches broad in the blade, and about 2 feet long, stiff, and with little spring in the handle ... Wooden racquets was played in the recess between the school outer wall and the entrance to the College ... College door was a 'let'. There was no ball-fagging for wooden racquets. Captain F. Markham (1903), *Recollections of a Town Boy at Westminster*

About wire racquets Captain Markham, at Westminster from 1849-55, wrote:

We used several balls, and the ball-fag had to retrieve all that went out of play, and to be ready to supply the man serving as required. When ball-fagging, you had the right of calling on any boy junior to yourself who came into Little Dean's Yard, and he had to take your place till he could spot some other unfortunate to relieve him. For this cause one was often tied to one's house till school-time, if a boy senior to one's self was doing ball-fag ... Ball and racquet when ordered, were supplied by an old gentleman called 'Ballman'; like most of our attendants he was not dignified with a surname.

Bat Fives

Bat Fives, a game gone and long forgotten, was played at many other schools, alongside hand (glove) fives. At Shrewsbury two new ball-courts were built in 1798. The bat was twenty-one inches long and four inches wide at its broadest. Bat Fives ended with the school's move up the hill in 1882. At Tonbridge the single wall fell down in 1893, and at Clifton, where a professional rackets player was engaged to improve 'a very popular game', the last singles competition was in 1915. Bat Fives was also played at Charterhouse – at Westminster it was called Racquets, but at Charterhouse it was Tennis, Leeds G.S., Bradfield, Sherborne ('ye fives place' 1675), Cheltenham, Marlborough, Radley and, no doubt, elsewhere. Fives often features violently in early school stories. The bat was used as a whippy implement of punishment, and the court or its vicinity was the accepted venue for bare-knuckle fights. At Shrewsbury

... the junior court ... was the recognised site for fights, which were watched by crowds of spectators seated on the steps and the retaining wall above it.

36. 'Little Dean's Yard, Westminster in 1845 ... Notable features of this picture are
... the boys playing racquets in the recess between School and College [Scholars],
and the Tudor "pepper-pot" caps on the South Transept of the Abbey [Now replaced
by Gothic pinnacles.],' John Field (1987), *The King's Nurseries.* 'Wooden racquets
was played in the recess between the school outer wall and the entrance to the
College ... College door was a "let",' Captain F. Markham (1903), *Recollections of a
Town Boy at Westminster 1849-1855* [Wooden racquets = Bat Fives]

37. Shrewsbury, The Old
School, 1811. The ball courts on
right were the venue for fights.
The school moved up to its
present site in 1882.

38. Hand Fives and Bat Fives,
Marlborough, 1849.

... the boys obsrved some sort of convention; there were seconds; and drinks usually, strange to say, water, afterwards. It was always said that Butler watched the fights from his window, he certainly turned a blind eye to them ... Edgar Montagu, who was at the School 1830-8, refers to one fight which became a legend,between two boys named Potter and Agnew ... which extended to fifty-two rounds. And these fights are described as having been 'fierce and frequent, amounting, it is said, to as many as seventy in one term and when few mornings passed without John Bandy making his appearance in the amphitheatre at nine o-clock to warn the spectators that time was up, and that they must go in for breakfast'. J.B. Oldham (1952), *A History of Shrewsbury School*

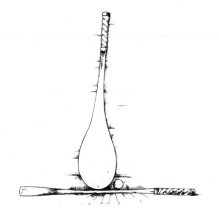

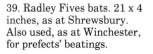

39. Radley Fives bats. 21 x 4
inches, as at Shrewsbury.
Also used, as at Winchester,
for prefects' beatings.

40. Radley in the 1890s. The flagged Bell Tower Fives Courts built in 1855. Later used for squash.

Eton

The game of Eton Fives has an affinity with Real Tennis in that both of them use a court which is imposed by the original playing area in which the game developed. At Eton this was against the Chapel wall, between two buttresses at the front of the court, and with a step down to a lower level for the back of the court; with the balustrade of the Chapel steps projecting into the left-hand side of the court a short distance behind the step. The game was originally played with bare hands, but with a harder ball gloves were introduced, and they also protect fingers and knuckles from the projections of the court.

The Chapel court was in use until the first new courts were built in 1840 ... During the first half of the 19th century the game gradually became popular at Eton ... Certain houses built more or less exact replicas of the Chapel court. In 1840 Dr Hawtrey, sometime Headmas-

41. Eton Fives. Taking advantage of
building features to invent a game.
Chapel steps court to left.

42. Chapel steps, Eton. The
balustrade of the steps projecting
into the court gave birth to the main
feature of the game.

ter of Eton, built the first block of Eton Fives courts four in number ...
suitably adapted.[1]

43. In 1894 Eton had 50
courts 'and finds them none
too many'. Today there are
only 15, but this is still the
biggest number anywhere.
Eton Fives courts can be
found in Switzerland,
Germany, Austria, Malaya,
Nigeria and Australia.

All later courts have been based on Dr Hawtrey's, and are mostly now covered. The Rules of Eton Fives were first published in 1877 and the first school match was Eton v. Harrow in 1885.

Modern Fives

A few fives-playing schools still keep to the rules of the game peculiar to themselves, but a majority have adopted Rugby Fives, probably because the courts are simplest to build. Many others play Eton Fives; and a minority have followed the Winchester Fives court with the single buttress. Unlike Eton and Rugby Fives, there is no Winchester Fives Association. Rugby Fives is the most energetic game with long rallies, though all three games fully exercise all parts of the body. Eton Fives, like Real Tennis, is the most complicated and most cerebral. It can only be played in doubles. Winchester Fives is similar to Rugby Fives, but the tactics are different, in that the buttress compels a division of partners front and back instead of left and right of the court, making singles a difficult game to play; but matches do take place between schools playing the two games and Winchester Fives players have taken part successfully in the Rugby Fives competitions.

Chapter 4

Cricket

The schools playing in the Lord's festival week (Eton, Harrow and Winchester) represented wealth, the nobility, and were linked to a large proportion, if not a majority, of both Houses of Parliament. The Public Schools week, coming towards the end of the London season, was thus an important event on the Victorian social calendar (and the Eton and Harrow match remained so at least up to the Second World War). The high profile of those playing in these two-day

44. Eton v. Harrow at Lord's 1864. Horses were later excluded from the ground.

holiday matches ensured that a majority of University 'Blues' came from the three schools. Other schools could not hope to compete in public interest with the Lord's Public Schools. However, probably in emulation, a lot of school cricket was played, and reports and full scores of matches appeared in *Bell's Life in London & Sporting Chronicle*. These were nearly all internal games or matches with local clubs. Interschool matches in term-time involved travel and absence from school.

In the 1850s there were more reports of interschool matches. Westminster and Charterhouse, very conscious of their status as public schools, played each other in 1850 and 1851. Westminster played Rugby in 1852, and Charterhouse deigned to play Marlborough at the end of the decade; but that was all. Both schools limited themselves to internal games or club matches, in particular with the two leading clubs, Marylebone and I Zingari. Rugby, a strong cricketing school, which played the Leicester county club annually, was more adventurous. Apart from the Westminster match in 1852, they played Marlborough a number of times at Lord's or the Oval, and Cheltenham. Marlborough and Cheltenham also met annually.

It was much easier for day schools to arrange matches, as they played at the week-ends, mostly on neutral grounds. In London, in the 1850s, Merchant Taylors' played St Paul's, King's College School (1829), then in the Strand, and University College School (1830) in

45. 'The Cricket Match at Tonbridge School 1851' by Charles Tattenhall Dodd, drawing master at the school. The Tudor buildings in the background were pulled down in 1864, and the old bat fives court behind the tree fell down in 1893. A number of cricketing counties are indebted to a particular school, as Derbyshire is to Repton and Worcestershire to Malvern. Some forty Old Tonbridgians have played for Kent; at present there are four on the county staff.

46. The second pavilion at Lord's was built in 1826 to replace the original one burnt down the year before. It was enlarged in 1865. It was replaced by the present pavilion in 1889.

Gower Street. The latter two schools had been founded together with the two Colleges of the University of London, as their junior departments. They played each other regularly at Lord's, both 1st and 2nd XIs on the same day. In London too Highgate met Kensington G.S. and Clapham G.S. In Yorkshire Leeds G.S. played Bingley, Bradford and Pocklington Grammar Schools. In East Anglia Bury G.S. played Ipswich G.S., and Felsted met K.E.S. Chelmsford. One of the oldest annual fixtures was between two more of the many grammar schools founded or re-founded in the brief reign of Edward VI, K.E.S. Birmingham and K.E.S. Bromsgrove. The former also played Shrewsbury in 1854 and Repton in 1859. Other regular fixtures were between Brighton and Tonbridge, and in 1859 Brighton also played Lancing; in Scotland between Edinburgh Academy, Glenalmond and Merchiston Castle; and in the south-west K.E.S. Sherborne and K.E.S. Bruton. In 1859 Queen Mary's G.S. Basingstoke played Wellington.

Lord's

The reader will be surprised to hear that the matches at Lord's in the 'fifties and 'sixties were mostly of no interest except to the players themselves. Scratch teams of amateurs against the Club with bowlers and such like comprised most of them ... Lord's was a heavy clay and badly drained ... The wickets at Lord's were fairly good, though sometimes for the less important matches they were terrible. The outfielding was always rough and treacherous ... There were no stands or fixed seats of any kind, nothing but the small old pavilion and a line of loose benches running part of the way round the ground, and these were but little occupied save at the more important matches. There were no 'boundaries'* except the pavilion, which stood on the site of the present one. None were required; they were regarded in those days, not

---

* Boundaries were introduced in 1866.

as a desirable aid to long scoring and a relief to the batsmen and fielders, but mere nuisances. The benches were not 'boundaries'; a fieldsman was supposed to be able to hop over a bench, while if the ball hit one, well, it was merely a 'rub of the green' ... 'Fivers' frequently, and occasionally 'Sixers', were run out at Lord's ... All over England runs were run out ... At Marlborough the match ground was and is a broad terrace raised at the top of a long, very gradual slope, on which all the lower games are played. A ball hit off the plateau to square leg, once it reached these slightly sloping clean shaven grounds, had great opportunities if hit hard enough ... The record was a 'tenner' ... Rev. J.F. Scobell, a curate in Devonshire, sent a thrill through the whole of the West Country making 41 in a single over of four balls – three 'tens' and an 'eleven' – all run out and no over-throws while playing against the Plymouth Garrison on their own ground. Edward Rutter[*] (1925), *Cricket Memories*

On 22 September 1850 a letter appeared in *Bell's Life* under the heading 'The Public School Matches', which was to initiate a long, acrimonious, futile and ultimately entertaining correspondence.

15 September 1850, Sir: There is a report current in these quarters that Winchester School will not contend again in the public school matches at Lord's. The Winchester have to contend against so many disadvantages that it is almost impossible to do so with any fair hope of success, and, as 'An Old Wykehamist' observed in your columns, each year they only add another stone to the heap of their disgrace. You, Mr Editor, will be able to learn from good authority whether the report that I have mentioned be correct; but I think it right thus early to put forward the claims of Rugby to the vacant place. Indeed I could hardly suppose that any other school would contest the honour. Eton and Harrow will no longer have any excuse for not playing Rugby ... H.L.W. (Rugby)

6 October 1850, Sir: ... I beg to inform you that Winchester has no intention whatever of retiring. In consequence of the refusal of the authorities to allow matches with other elevens to take place on our ground, we have not noticed the necessity of giving up the loose style of playing which belongs to this place, and the consequence of that has hitherto been that we have annually been beaten by both the other public schools for the last six years. We began to see our error last year, and we sent up a steadier eleven than we had done for a long time before ... There is one other subject to which I must beg to allude. I mean the letter which appeared a short time since in your paper, in which Westminster, though not yet equal to Harrow or Eton, was pronounced quite a match for Winchester. We receive that notice as a sort of challenge and, as such, we answer that if it is renewed next year, the Winchester Eleven will be happy to play the Eleven of Westminster on their own ground before the matches at Lord's commence. A Member of Winchester College

6 October 1850, Sir: ... Whilst staying in Marlbro' ... when I was talking to one of the Marlborough Coll First Eleven and asked him why

---

[*] He was at Rugby 1853-62 and played for Middlesex 1868-76.

they did not play with Rugby? he replied, we sent a challenge to Rugby, and the answer they returned was, 'We don't play private schools'. Allow me to inform the Rugbeans that Marlborough is no more a private school than Rugby. If anything like a private school is to be found in either, I should think it was Rugby; and I think it is a great pity that if Winchester does retire from the Eton and Harrow, that the Winchester, Marlborough and Cheltenham, or Westminster Colleges do not play next season their friendly matches at Lord's during their holidays, as the Eton, Harrow, and Rugby will henceforth most likely do …
A Veteran Rugbean

Immediately following the above was the first letter from an authoritative source:

6 October 1850, Sir: The Rugbean (H.L.W.) who commenced this discussion lost sight of the important fact that, even though Winchester should ever think of retiring from an uneven contest, Rugby could never take its place, from the utter impossibility of collecting its eleven a month after the commencement of the holidays …
J.H.C. (Head of the Rugby Eleven)

47. Cricket at Rugby 1862. In early days many teams wore coloured shirts. The Rugby XI's duck-egg blue shirts are the only remaining example, if one discounts the modern 'pyjama' game.

(The Lord's matches were played at the start of the Eton and Harrow holidays, but in the middle of the Winchester – and Rugby holidays.)

13 October 1850, Sir: ... I beg on the part of the Marlborough College Eleven, most distinctly to state that no challenge has ever been sent to Rugby from Marlborough, with the consent of the Eleven.
T.S., Hon. Sec. to the Marlborough College

20 October 1850, Sir: Among the numerous letters inserted in your paper ... it is stated that Rugby wished Winchester to retire from the contest ... in which it has been beaten for the last few years. Now this may be traced to two circumstances; first that Dr Moberly, the present head master of Winchester College, has refused the old custom of having a professional bowler to bowl to the Wykehamists during their hours of vacation;[1] the second is that Winchester College is much emptier than it has been for some time, and that the players are much smaller than those of Eton and Harrow ...
Amicus Famae Wintonensis

20 October 1850, Sir: ... Fearing lest silence should be misconstrued, I shall be obliged by your inserting this, although I should have preferred taking no notice of so absurd a proposal as that which he makes. The 'Veteran Rugbean' appears to have entirely overlooked the possibility of the public schools, so considerately mentioned in his category, not wishing to engage with the establishments at Marlborough and Cheltenham ... I do not wish for a moment to disparage the merits of those schools ... but I must beg to state that it is useless to imagine that Westminster will ever consent to join in any such arrangement, or to depart from her long established rule of not playing any other than public schools or recognised clubs.
W.G.A. (Captain of the Westminster XI)

3 November 1850, Sir: During the excitement prevalent among the public schools, relative to cricket, I think that King's College, London should not be forgotten, which, though perhaps not possessing such advantages as the rest, may by a little more application to that noble sport be nearer on a parallel, if not with Rugby and Harrow, at any rate with some of those who have not yet any yearly competition. Why not then let King's College play yearly matches? ...
A Friend to All

10 November 1850, Sir: ... Rugby is as much entitled to play in the public school matches as Harrow. Old Lawrence Sheriffe was probably as jolly a fellow as John Lyon, though p'raps not so fierce. 2nd, The Westminster School Eleven, or rather the captain, states that they never play any other than public schools; that clearly accounts for their not shining so brilliantly in the cricket department; for mighty few matches in my recollection ... have they played with the public schools. Let me then propose a match for them, as to contend against Rugby or Marlborough would be infra dig, viz., Twenty-two of Westminster School v. The One-legged Greenwich Pensioners ... to come off during the Exhibition of 1851.
From an Old Rugbean

(In 1851 Winchester was allowed to engage the veteran William

Lillywhite to bowl to them. Results were immediate, as Winchester won both Lord's matches, after five years of continuous defeat. Despite this the acrimony of 1850 intensified in 1851.)

13 July 1851, Sir: In one of your papers last autumn ... the captain of the Winchester Eleven stated that they would be happy to play Westminster this year, but now when the time comes they refuse to play ... If there is any reason for the backing out of the match, the captain ought not to have accepted the challenge last year ...
An Old Westminster

17 August 1851, Sir: ... Some time ago, I forget the year, some gentlemen of King's College School thought proper to send a challenge to the Westminster Eleven, which the latter declined ... the reason being given ... that they never played other than public schools and recognised clubs ... This course, so obviously the only one that could possibly have been taken, ... seems nevertheless to have left behind it some degree of rancour in the breasts of the students in the Strand, which even lapse of time has not removed. For, on what seems to them a just retribution falling on the devoted head of Westminster, we find it breaking forth most vigorously in triumph at the circumstance that the Winchester Eleven refused to play that of Westminster.
A Young Old Westminster

17 August 1851, Sir: A correspondent in your last number expresses a hope that the Westminster Gentlemen very soon may play with the Public Schools at Lord's; but have not the Westminsters already commenced an annual match with the Gentlemen of the Charterhouse? the Charterhouse being a celebrated public school when Harrow was known only for its 'visible church' – for Harrow, with her non-aristocratical sister, Rugby, were only considered as village schools for the first hundred and fifty years after their foundation. About twenty-five years ago the Wykehamists joined Eton and Harrow in their annual match, Westminster no longer being the aristocratical school she was during the last century. It is *from this time*, I believe, that the Wykehamists of the present day date Winchester being a public school ...
An Old Carthusian

17 August 1851, Sir: Westminster and Rugby it appears are anxious to play at Lord's. Why should they not? Unfortunately the former cannot be admitted to the cricketing competition of its three old rivals (and fellows in the now nearly forgotten school saw),[2] for that would involve six matches in place of three, and keep all the elevens in London for nearly a fortnight. But let Rugby, on the strength of its new celebrity, challenge Westminster; let Westminster put its pride in its pipe, smoke it, and accept the challenge (it has already played Charterhouse) ...
Verbum Sap

24 August 1851, Sir: ... The 'Old Carthusian' has wagged his tail at Eton, snarled at Harrow, barked at Winchester, put his finger in the pie to try and create a quarrel between Westminster and Winchester, and blown a penny trumpet for Charterhouse ... I will conclude with a little parting advice from an old Carthusian, the immortal Addison,

48. 'Fields', Vincent Square, 1845. Five minutes from the school. At Westminster, Tuttle (Tothill) Fields had long been the boys' playing fields, but at the beginning of the 19th century they were enclosed so that they might be let for building. However [in 1810] as the result of an appeal by the school, ten acres were preserved as playing fields for it.' H.J.C. Blake (1831), *Reminiscences of Eton*. William Vincent, former Head Master, then Dean, marked off the ten acres with a plough and surrounded it with a trench.

'There is nothing that more betrays a base ungenerous spirit than the givings of secret stabs to a man's reputation'.
An Old Wykehamist

7 September 1851, Sir: Do you not think that sufficient has been said and written on the subject of public school matches, and that it would be a very good thing for all parties if no more were published ... as it not only keeps up a spirit of jealousy ... but it also brings forward a display of ill-feeling, which is anything but creditable to those engaged in the disputes? ...
P.T.D.

28 September 1851, Sir: I and other old public school men are much disgusted at the large correspondence which takes up your valuable columns concerning 'our matches' ... It does ... seem to us that it is a very hard case that three elevens, consisting of the sons of noblemen and gentlemen of this realm, cannot meet on the 'neutral ground of Lord's' to have a trial of skill without that said trial being the cause of unpleasant remarks and invidious strictures. Such remarks and strictures will do much towards stopping these matches altogether ...
From an Old Etonian

Westminster had drawn with Charterhouse in 1850, and won by 8 wickets in 1851. Next year, 1852, they met Rugby, at last, at Vincent Square. For Westminster it was a crushing defeat. Rugby scored 114 and 129, with 43 and 46 extras, mostly byes, in either innings, and dismissed Westminster for 19 and 11 (including 4 byes). Westminster were missing their best player who was unfit, and two other members of the Eleven had refused to play, for an undisclosed reason, but presumably because they disapproved of the match.

Winchester continued to play the Lord's matches until 1854, after which 'the complaints of parents at the expense and the dangers of boys being a week in London in the holidays' reinforced Dr Moberly's prejudices and he brought them to an end. The decision was deplored by Wykehamists of all ages. 'The Warden summoned us College Prefects to announce to us this momentous fact. The indignation seemed almost to threaten rebellion.'[3] Of these matches played at Lord's over three decades Winchester won 11 and lost 13 to Harrow; and won 10, lost 14 and tied once with Eton. Lillywhite's coaching improved the record considerably, Winchester winning six of their last eight matches. There was only one further century in this series of 49 matches with Eton and Harrow, again by a Wykehamist. Totals under one hundred in a completed innings were more common than

49. Winchester v. Eton 1864. A half holiday was given. 'Half the Eton boys come over by railway and are entertained in Hall. At London, where, besides the eleven, there probably would not be half-a-dozen present'. R.B. Mansfield (1870), *School-Life at Winchester College*

50. At the Eton and Harrow
Cricket Match 1881.

those over a hundred (90 to 84). In 1834 Winchester beat Harrow by
one wicket when all four innings were in the forties. Winchester
continued to play Eton, alternately home and away, but the Harrow
match was discontinued, the authorities probably feeling that one
school match in term-time was distraction enough. The Winchester
Eleven to this day is nostalgically known as 'Lord's'. At Eton too Dr
Goodford (1853-62) had reservations. In 1856 and 1857 he barred the
Etonians from appearing at Lord's in the holidays; the Harrow match
played in the latter year was between boys who had left school.

The departure of Winchester led to a renewal of support for
Rugby's case for inclusion, but to no effect. In 1858 an Eton v. Radley
race at Henley, which took place just after the Regatta, was the cause
of a further plea.

> 1858, Sir: As an Etonian, of course I rejoice that Eton has beaten
> Radley at Henley; but let us hear no more of Eton not being able to pull
> a match, or play at cricket against this or that school, *because they are
> not public schools* so called. What right has Radley, of five years'
> standing, to be challenged by Eton when they [Eton] will not play
> Rugby at cricket, simply because it has not been the custom, and it is
> not deemed right to play any school but Harrow or Winchester? How-
> ever we must hope for more sensible action for the future, and as the
> Rugbians leave school in June, let the Etonians ask them to come and
> play in the shooting fields. All will rejoice to see the match, and a

liberal system begin at Eton of playing any school who think they can
pluck away the Etonian laurel ...
One who has been in the XI at Eton, and loved her well.

Non-Public School Cricket

So much emphasis on school cricket seems out of proportion; but in
the 1850s the amateur game as a whole predominated – in the
sporting press at least. *Bell's Life* published full match scores from a
multitude of local clubs, a few of which employed one or a pair of
professional bowlers; university colleges 1st and 2nd XIs; schools,
including internal games; military garrisons; London hospitals; the
Gentlemen of Surrey and Sussex etc; wandering clubs such as I
Zingari and Free Foresters; and from Lord's M.C.C.'s mix of amateurs and professionals. For much of the readership Oxford & Cambridge and Eton & Harrow ranked alongside Gentlemen v. Players
a d North v. South as the most important games of all.

Counties met seldom, even though such matches had been played
for well over a century. Kent v. London in 1719 was the first 'County
Match', and Surrey played Middlesex in 1730. Yet not until 1835 did
a northern county play a southern, when Notts played and beat
Sussex. There were then no county clubs with a constitution and
membership, representative county sides being selected from local
clubs; no strict county qualifications; and no official county championship – nor was there to be until the 1890s. In the '50s only Surrey,
Kent and Sussex feature at all regularly. Instead, the leading professionals organised themselves into touring teams. The most famous
were the All-England Eleven formed in 1846, and in 1852 the United
All-England Eleven, a breakaway group dissatisfied with their share

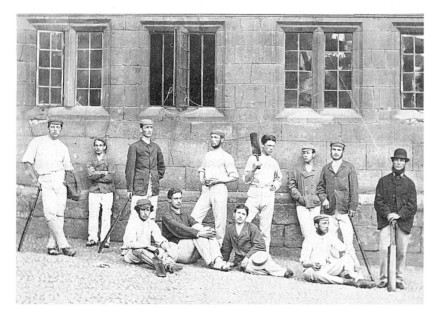

51. The Shrewsbury School
Cricket XI of 1868 together
with a pro, outside the old
school building.

of the takings. Recruited mainly from the northern counties, they travelled all over the country, playing three-day matches against odds, for a guaranteed fee, with such as XVI Sussex Amateurs, XX Gentlemen of Hampshire, XXII 'Bona Fide' Irishmen with Lawrence, or XXII of Walsall & District (with Grundy and Slinn) – two of their professional bowlers. The great touring sides attracted good gates, and when they finally met at Lord's huge crowds came to watch. They proved effective missionaries in bringing cricket to remoter parts of Britain, and in unearthing local talent.

By the 1860s the interest in cricket that the touring sides had helped to foster stirred the counties to establish themselves. The Surrey County Cricket Club had been formed in 1845, when the Kennington Oval was first opened. Now other counties belatedly followed their example, Sussex in 1857, Yorkshire in 1863, and in 1864 Lancashire and Middlesex, (who became M.C.C.'s lodgers at Lord's from 1876). The sporting press encouraged competition by publishing unofficial championship tables; but the official County Championship had to wait for another thirty years. Eventually, the touring teams, having served their turn, disbanded, but not before bad feeling between northern and southern professionals led, in 1865, to the defection of the latter to form a third side, the United South of England Eleven.

The 1850s and 1860s were also the decades when cricket became international. The first overseas tour was undertaken in 1859, across the Atlantic to Canada and the United States. The first tour to Australia followed closely in 1861. By this time cricket was being played all over the world, and not just in the Colonies. In the 1850s and 1860s *Bell's Life* published details of matches in Montreal and in Constantinople, in St Petersburg and in St Helena, from the West Indies to the East Indies, from China to Peru. As happened with football three or four decades later, British people working or resident abroad formed cricket clubs. *Bell's Life* reported Florence v. Leghorn, Lyons v. Geneva, Jerez v. Seville, Westphalia v. Bonn, Champs Elysées v. Brussels, France v. Germany in Homburg, and England beating Yorkshire in the Charlottenburg Hippodrome, Berlin. All the players were British. Unlike football, cricket has never caught the imagination of continental Europeans, although some famous names in European football started out as Cricket and Football Clubs.

The British Empire

Where cricket did put down strong roots was in the Empire. Cricket, like trade, followed the flag, and the agency responsible for this was the Army. The Duke of Wellington's dictum that 'the Battle of Waterloo was won on the playing-fields of Eton' may be apocryphal, but in 1841 he recognised the importance of cricket in strengthening both muscle and morale, when he directed that every military barracks

52. Clifton College in 1867. Clifton is one of the two schools from which the largest number of boys pass direct into the R.M.A., Woolwich, and R.M.C., Sandhurst. 35 Old Cliftonian officers served in the late campaign on the Indian Frontier, of whom 22 were mentioned in despatches and 6 recommended for the Distinguished Service Order. The connection of the school with Egypt and the Soudan is hardly less memorable (1898). Henry Newbolt (1898), *The Island Race*

should have its cricket ground. Regiments in permanent garrisons wherever the map was pink played internal matches – Officers v. Sergeants, Sergeants v. Corporals, or all ranks against another regiment. When the opponents were a local side, the regimental team was usually made up of officers.

Where the Army couldn't go, the Royal Navy obliged. St Petersburg v. H.M.S. St George and Chanticleer, Lima v. H.M.S. Clio, Batavia v. H.M.S. Ferooz, Valparaiso v. H.M.S. Portland and Amphitrite. In Corfu the Officers of the Garrison played the Officers of the Fleet. Corfu ceased to be British in 1864, but cricket is still played there.

During the 1850s Canada played the United States annually in Toronto or New York. In 1855 there was no match as 'several players were ordered with their regiments to the Crimea'. The previous year at Varna Camp, Scutari, on the Bosphorus, the Fusilier Guards played the 49th Regiment. 'Two matches were played previous to our departure for more active service. The sudden order for the brigade of Guards to embark prevented either of the matches being finished', but the scores were provided to *Bell's Life* nonetheless. In the Baltic, in an abortive expedition under Sir Charles Napier to the Gulf of Finland and Kronstadt, the island fortress of St Petersburg, H.M.S. Royal George (mostly wardroom) lost by 9 wickets to H.M.S. Cressy (mostly lower deck) on Nargen Island, five miles off Reval (now Tallinn, Estonia). The report ended: 'An eleven selected from these ships together hope to have a more even game by meeting an eleven chosen from the remaining nine ships of the squadron. P.S. Aland is taken with a loss of 13 killed; 3500 men having been taken prisoners, and are on their way to England.' Finally, in the Crimea itself the 12th Lancers played the 21st Fusiliers 'on the height before Sebas-

53a. E.F.S. Tylecote (Clifton).

53b. C.L. Townsend (Clifton).

VITAI LAMPADA

There's a breathless hush in the Close to-night
Ten to make and the match to win
A bumping pitch and a blinding light,
An hour to play and the last man in.
And it's not for the sake of a ribboned coat,
Or the selfish hope of a season's fame,
But his Captain's hand on his shoulder smote
'Play up! play up! and play the game!'

The sand of the desert is sodden red, –
Red with the wreck of a square that broke; –
The Gatling's jammed and the Colonel dead,
And the regiment blind with dust and smoke.
The river of death has brimmed his banks,
And England's far, and Honour a name,
But the voice of a schoolboy rallies the ranks:
'Play up! play up! and play the game!'

This is the word that year by year,
While in her place the School is set,
Every one of her sons must hear,
And none that hears it dare forget.
This they all with a joyful mind
Bear through life like a torch in flame,
And falling fling to the host behind –
'Play up! play up! and play the game!'

Henry Newbolt (1898), *The Island Race*

53c. A.E.J. Collins, 628 not out.
A.E.J.Collins was born in India,
and he returned there after he
had joined the Royal Engineers.
On November 11, 1914 Captain
Collins was shot and killed in
the First Battle of Ypres.

53d. W. Bounsall (Clifton).

topol, but a regular Crimea thunderstorm coming on in the afternoon it was impossible to play it out'.

Close of the 19th century

In the latter part of the century there was no great increase in the number of inter-school matches. For most schools one or perhaps two were enough. Lord's remained a magnet. From 1867 Westminster and Charterhouse played there annually until Charterhouse's move from the City to Godalming in 1872. Rugby and Marlborough had met variously at Lord's, the Oval and Middlesex's first ground in Islington, before settling down at Lord's in 1871, where they met annually for the next hundred years. For much of the 1870s some outstanding Uppingham Elevens played Surrey at the Oval and M.C.C. at Lord's. Also in the 1870s Rossall, the leading northern proprietary school, isolated from competition on the Fylde coast, came down to London to play Haileybury at the Oval and Sherborne at Lord's, and in a second expedition met Surrey and M.C.C. In 1894 Cheltenham began the long series against Haileybury at Lord's with a 1 run victory. Twenty years later, in 1914, M.C.C. invited Clifton and Tonbridge to play their annual fixture at Lord's. These two strong cricketing schools had first met in 1899. This was the year when 13 year old Arthur Edward Jeune Collins (see illustration 53c), in a Clifton Junior School house match, scored 628 not out (in a total of 836, including 183 for the last wicket). This is still the highest individual score recorded anywhere.

Chapter 5

Football

The Eton and Westminster boat races on the Thames were reported at length in the sporting and national press; and as we have seen, full scores of school and other cricket matches were appearing regularly in *Bell's Life in London*, the leading sporting weekly. However 'It is curious to note that in 1860 besides the Universities and Public Schools, only two [football] clubs, the Dingley Dell and Crusaders, appeared in the sporting papers as playing first-class matches, and in *The Field* of 1862 hardly any mention is made of the game.' [1]

In the first half of the 19th century football is treated almost as past history. Joseph Strutt, the antiquary, in his *Pastimes of the People of England* published in 1801, wrote: 'Football formerly much in vogue among the common people, of late years seems to have fallen into disrepute and is but little practised.' In *The Boy's Treasury of Sports and Pastimes* of 1844 Football is given twelve lines, fewer than Fives, Golf, Hurling, Rackets and Stoolball: 'Foot-ball was once a popular old English game ... It was formerly a favourite Shrove Tuesday game in many towns of England'. The 18th-century Enclosure Acts, by fencing in the wastes and commons and depopulating the countryside, largely killed off village football. In the towns the traditional Shrove Tuesday holiday games were progressively banned by the increasingly effective powers of law and order. In Derby the parishes of St Peter's and All Saints met annually in the streets of the town, 500 a-side, before large crowds of spectators and boarded up windows. (The origin of 'a local Derby'.) In 1847 the Mayor read the Riot Act, two troops of Dragoons stood ready, and the crowd dispersed for the last time. Only in Yorkshire's broad acres did 'the old English rustic game of football' appear still to have a significant hold. An Etonian wrote in 1831: 'I cannot consider the game of football as being at all gentlemanly. It is a game which the common people of Yorkshire are particularly partial to, the tips of their shoes being heavily shod with iron; and frequently death has been known to ensue from the severity of the blows inflicted thereby.'[2] *The Yorkshireman* 17 October 1841: 'We are happy to see that the old English diversion of football is once more beginning to revive. A capital match was played at Eton College ... between Collegers and Oppidans ... We hope the other counties will follow the good example.'

In Scotland, however, football was still being played, at least in the beginning of the 19th century: 'In 1815 we read of a great football

54. Football at Rugby, 1845. Early scrums were stand-up mêlées with either side trying to hack the ball through (different from hacking down). Heeling put everyone in the scrum off-side. At Winchester a scrum was a hot – also at Bradfield. At Eton, Westminster, Uppingham, Rossall, a bully – at Eton 'any episode of violent activity' was a rouge – as at Charterhouse; at Stonyhurst, Charterhouse, Marlborough, Cheltenham, a squash; at Downside a shindy; at Sherborne a grovel – also used at Marlborough for a maul in goal; at Tonbridge a gutter; at Radley a pudding; at Repton and Shrewsbury a scrimmage – also squash; at Rugby a scrummage. All very descriptive words.

match being played at Carterhaugh in Ettrick Forest, between the Ettrick men and the men of Yarrow, the one party backed by the Earl of Home, and the other by Sir Walter Scott, then Sheriff of the forest. The latter wrote a couple of songs in honour of the occasion, from one of which we quote a verse –

> Then strip lads, and to it, though sharp be the weather;
> And if by mischance you should happen to fall,
> There are worse things in life than a tumble on heather,
> And life is itself but a game of football.
> M. Shearman and J.E. Vincent (1885),
History of Foot-Ball for Five Centuries

In the 1850s virtually all school football matches reported in the press were internal (e.g. North Side of Chapel v. South, Sixth v. The Rest, Monosyllables v. Polysyllables, Tall v. Short, A.B.C.D.E.F.G. v. the World, Light Hair v. Dark) or against teams made up of Old Boys. In this regard Radley was exceptionally fortunate, in the 1850s and early 1860s perhaps unique. Oxford college footballers, starved of their game, were near enough and ready enough to come out by drag to play according to Radley Rules.[3] Between 1857 and 1880 there were 122 of these foreign matches (W 44, D 37, L 41, GF 97, GA 130). Eton too played matches against teams from the Universities and from various military establishments, but these were hardly foreign matches, since both types of institution were brimming with Etonians. In 1855 there was a football match 'In the Field' (doubly so) in the Crimea between the Guards and the Cavalry Division, 'the Elevens on both sides consisting entirely of old Etonians' (1 – 1). How to arrange a match with another school, when each school had its own rules and conventions? The differences and difficulties are illustrated in the following extracts:

Durham: Once under way it was considered unmanly to pass the ball rather than run on until overwhelmed.[4]

Forest: The road skirting the Common was counted as a touch-line and the big chestnut trees along the side were then 'in-play' and allies of a tricky player ... pointed out that in his day it helped to produce two-footed players by players staying on the same side of the field when they changed ends.

King's, Canterbury: Before 1872 all games were played on the Green Court and, in those days, many a good player learned to sidestep and swerve as he avoided the trees and railings around the Green Court to score under the posts. 1872 Affiliated to R.F.U.[5]

Bradford G.S.: The School, aroused at length to a sense of the disgraceful condition of its games, has secured a field, formed a Club, and played a match. What is to be its future? Is it to rise to its former position or are we to lose for ever the glory and fame of our Football Club? The answer must depend on the action of the parents and of the boys. Many of the former, who hate the very name of football, hinder us by absolutely forbidding their sons to play ... Skill has taken the place of brute force, and the danger instead of being increased is considerably diminished. Thirty years ago, for instance, the townships of Clayton and Clayton Heights were at daggers drawn: every Christmas they had a football match. All modern notions about touchdowns, tries and mauls were unknown, but with what a result! A few minutes after the start the ball was usually lost sight of, the rival teams tried to kick each other off the field, and carried their animosity to such a pitch that they fastened spikes into the tops of their boots to add to the unpleasantness of the attack. Yorkshiremen in general and the Bradford Yorkshiremen in particular delight to associate with it, as an inevitable result, visions of broken arms, collar bones and funeral hearses. It is no criterion for the parents to visit some of the matches in the district of Bradford, where the language used is not the most refined, where every point is disputed, where free fights repeatedly take place ... The boys themselves, however, must chiefly be blamed for the decline of the Football Club: they have shown themselves utterly devoid of public spirit ... many truly deserve the disagreeable name of 'stew-pots'. This year out of a school of 450 only 60 have as yet condescended to join us. *Bradfordian* 1878-9

Lancing: I played scratch football with the Westminster Scholars and

55. Football on Green in
Dean's Yard, Westminster,
1845.

so got a more civilised football. When I returned to Lancing as a master
... I had a chat with the Captain. The first thing I fell upon was the
crowding of all the forwards on the leading forward ... so I made Rule
I – fixed places for all the forwards with passing the ball from one to
the other. You should have seen the faces of our opponents, a sort of
'Where do I come in?' look. J. Spencer Walker (1868-72) [Lancing
produced 7 internationals for England in the 1880s.]

Westminster (1850s): The real Westminster football was the game in
'green' – that is, in Great Dean's yard. It was indeed a general game,
for every boy had to play. Attendance in 'green' was compulsory in the
half before Christmas ... The goals were at top and bottom of 'green' ...
about 20 yards wide; the ball, to score a goal, had to pass at any height
between two trees at either end, and had to hit the rails or pass over
them. The small boys, the duffers, and the funk-sticks were the goal-
keepers, 12 or 15 at each end, and were spaced out across this wide
space; if any fellow who was playing out showed any sign of 'funk', or
failed to play up, he was packed off into goals at once, not only that day,
but as a lasting degradation ...

The 'scis' or 'skies' supposedlly from Volsci [see *Coriolanus*], were
challenged when they dared to set foot upon the Green or when they
refused to throw back a ball that had been kicked off during a game
(coal-heavers, draymen, butcher boys and carriers asserted right to
cross Dean's Yard at all times). General skirmishes seemed to be the
preferred form of exercise.[6]

56. The Eton Wall Game (1890). The most esoteric of the dozen different football codes being played to-day. It is confined to Eton and to its 118 yard wall bordering a 5 yard strip of grass, turned to thick mud when wet. Ten a-side. A static game with the half-sized soccer ball worked along the wall by the bully. No handling.No forward passing or heeling. One goal is a door in an end wall, the other end has no wall and goal is marked on a tree (off picture). Mainly played by College, who have an annual match with the Oppidans on St Andrew's Day. The game may derive from 'Passage Football' – cf. Charterhouse's old game in Cloisters. The wall on the Slough Road was built in 1717 so the game in its present form cannot be older than that; but it may be the oldest football game now being played. The other codes – all originating in the English-speaking world – are The Eton Field Game, Winchester, Harrow, Association, Rugby Union, Rugby League, Gaelic, Australian Rules, American College, American and Canadian Football. The very similar North American codes developed through the Universities: first Princeton Rules, similar to Association, 1867, then Rugby at Harvard, Yale and Princeton in the 1870s, and in 1880 Walter C. Camp of Yale abolished the scrum and made other changes, to give birth to a new game.

Magdalen College School, Oxford: The St Edward's match was dropped after a serio-comic incident in 1880-1. Magdalen committed the gaffe of 'heeling the ball out of the scrummage', thereby winning the game by one goal and two touchdowns to nil. St Edward's claimed that heeling out was illegal, and wrote to the Secretary of the Rugby Union, who, however, replied that he was 'sorry to say that it was allowable'.[7]

Marlborough (Before 1865): There was, of course, absolutely nothing in the shape of passing. When a player was collared, he was supposed to be bound to have the ball down, but not infrequently he had to be 'scragged' into submission; and after the ball was actually grounded he

57. The Cloister in 1894 after Charterhouse had moved to Godalming (in 1872).
'Football was of two kinds. On dry days the game was played in Under Green under
Association rules; on wet days in Cloisters ... The Cloister, paved with smooth
flagstones, but roughly constructed with sharp, jagged flint at its sides, was about
70 yards long, 9 feet wide, and 12 feet high ... On Wednesday afternoons a written
notice "All Fags to be in Cloisters at 2.30", used to be posted up ... At the appointed
time the Fags would assemble, and take up their position twenty strong at each end
of Cloisters; the Gownboy Fags at the door leading into their own House; the
Rest-of-School Fags at the south door ... The boys of the higher forms would then
range themselves down Cloisters ... The ball very soon got into one of the
buttresses, when a terrific squash would be the result, some 50 or so boys huddled
together, vigorously "rouging", kicking and shoving to extricate the ball. A skilful
player feeling that he had the ball in front of his legs, would patiently bide his time,
until, perceiving an opportunity, he would dextrously work out the ball and rush
wildly with it down Cloisters ... The squash would then dissolve and go in pursuit.
Now was the time for the pluck and judgment of the Fags ... One of the foremost
Fags would rush out and engage the onset of the dribbling foe, generally to be sent
sprawling head over heels for five yards along the stones. It served a purpose,
however, for it not only gave his side time to come up, but also his fellow fags
encouragement to show a close and firm front. If the boy with the ball happened to
be well backed up by his own Houses, they would launch themselves right into the
middle of the Fags, when a terrific scrimmage would ensue. The Fags would strive
their utmost to prevent the ball being driven through, and hammer away with fists
at hands grasping the corners of the wall to obtain a better purchase for scoring.
One of these scrummages sometimes lasted three-quarters of an hour. Shins would
be kicked black and blue; jackets and other articles of clothing almost torn to
shreds; and Fags trampled under foot. At the end, amid wild shouts of "through,
through", nearly the whole contending mass would collapse on the ground, when the
ball would be discovered under a heap of prostrate antagonists, and more or less the
worse for the fray ... The game in Cloisters was frequently so rough that delicate
fags would have given their most cherished possessions to have been let off
attendance thereat. Some, indeed, used to shirk the obligation in the meanest and
most contemptible manner by paltry excuses'. E.P. Eardley-Wilmot and E.C.
Streatfield (1895), *Charterhouse Old & New*

could keep his hand upon it, and thus hold it dead until a 'squash' or scrimmage was formed round him. Either by law or received custom, however, the ball might be held up within a measurable distance of the opponents' goal-line; and if the squash could be then forced over the line, the next proceeding was to engage in a 'grovel' on the ground. To an outsider a grovel must have presented a most grotesque spectacle, formed as it was of wriggling, writhing figures, with interlacing legs and arms, for all the world like a mass of mammoth worms, who struggled to prevent, or secure, a 'touchdown' or 'try', and who only dropped off one by one as they lost touch of the ball. These grovels lasted sometimes as long as ten minutes, till one or other of the captains of the sides gave up the contest.[8]

58. A Tonbridge Football XIII c. 1869. A letter in the *Tonbridgian* 1858: 'At other schools they have divisions of football corresponding to our elevens at cricket ... I suggest, therefore, that this school should have divisions or classes and that as the school consists of almost exactly 170, I suggest that a "twenty", a "fifty", and a "hundred" would be the best numbers.' The suggestion must have been taken up, because two grounds today are named 'The Fifty' and 'The Hundred', though they are not the original ones. Another letter at the time of this photograph 'remarks on the "needless ferocity" of Tonbridge football. Visiting teams have been overheard describing it as a "dirty game", and hinting that they will not visit again', D.C. Somervell (1947), *History of Tonbridge School*. Tonbridge was one of the first schools to join the newly-born Rugby Football Union.

Tonbridge: We played football on the gravel playground, thereby encouraging several respectable trades including that of the sticking-plaster maker, and enjoyed 'the glory and the gutter' in substantial form. The old playground was bounded by fences. Along the fences on either side was a stone gutter, and when at hockey or at football the leather got into this, there was a rush, a lawless scrummage, and a good deal of very lively shinning. In the fence along the lane were several gaps known as 'hospitals' because, after a gutter, players were apt to sit in them to examine and nurse their damaged shins. Our hockey and football were played in primitive style – two unorganised mobs hitting or kicking, up and down towards the goals, represented by the gates. We had only one rule that I remember, and that corresponded to the 'offside' of this more scientific age. The kick-off was from goal and then the sides charged each other like South African Impis [i.e. Zulu or Matabele war-bands.] Albany de Fonblanque (1842-6)[9]

Uppingham: In 1864 and 1865 cups were presented for house matches in football and cricket; up till now games had been concocted from strange-sounding sides within the School: 'Those with an R in their names v. The Rest.' Hence the story of Thring's anger when he discovered a proposed game posted on the boards as 'Those who have been flogged by Mr Thring v. Those who have not.' 'Ha!' he said, as he ran his pencil down the list, 'if that game takes place, all the players will be on the same side'.[10]

Harrow: Football till towards the 1820s was merely a kind of kick about in the Bill Yard, the great feat being to kick the ball right over the building. But by the 1830s, Harrow footer had developed on the hilly part of the cricket field ... Even more than now [1936] it was a good game for keeping little boys in their place, for they were all shoved into Base [goal], where they either stood shivering cold, or when the rush came were found lying on their backs in the mud ... The players went straight up to Bill without changing or washing and their dirty state made them almost indistinguishable when they answered their names. After that it was the custom to repair either to one of the public houses, e.g. The Crown & Anchor, or to one of the tuckshops to which tumblers of punch could be carried across on trays.[11]

K.C.S., Wimbledon then in the Strand: 1867-71. The concrete school yard was, I should think, as much like a prison yard as one could make it, and during a period of nearly 5 years I never knew the boys to indulge, during the quarter of an hour break and the half hour at one o'clock, in any pastime other than that of kicking about indiscriminately a piece of wood.[12]

Radley: It was in 1866 in a match with the Oxford Old Etonians that the Etonians claimed, as an indulgence, a momentary lapse to Eton rules and rouges; as a consequence a pudding [scrum] was formed, and one of them (Holbech) commenced 'crawling' with the ball. We believe that in the Eton rules 'crawling' though allowed, is, or was, accompanied with such maltreatment of the 'crawler' as to render it a practical impossibility; in this case, however, owing to the ignorance, or forbearance of our team, the crawler continued his grovelling career, until he finally emerged triumphant on the side nearest our goal. The scene of

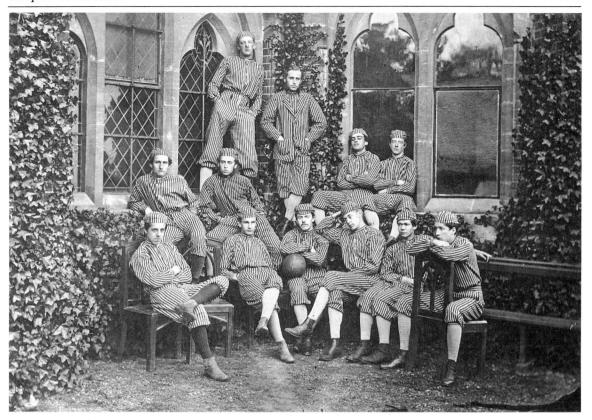

59. The Harrow Football Team of 1867 'clad in wonderful black and magenta garments, a rather middle-Victorian theme of colour ... The usual formation is 2 backs, 5 centre forwards, 2 right and 2 left wings. The ball is larger than the Association ball and heavier; it is shaped like a church hassock, with rounded ends and sides. The goals are called "bases" marked by high poles [no crossbar] ... One of the great acts in the game is that of "giving yards" to your own side at the right moment; that is turning round and kicking a gentle catch to someone on your own side who is not in front of you. This is by no means an easy task with a heavy muddy ball in the face of a vigilant enemy', J. Fischer Williams (1901), *Harrow*. By shouting 'Yards' the holder of the ball can then take three paces and kick the ball unimpeded – if near to them, through the poles to obtain a base. Footballers are still 'capped' and are sometimes given a cap, but they no longer wear it when playing.

confusion and scuffling between the rival teams whilst the process continued is beyond description (the performance, by the way, occupied nearly 20 minutes).[13]

Clifton (1897): More than 20 years ago it was an act of high treason to put down one's head in the scrummage, and if anybody did so, an opponent would probably remind him of this breach of etiquette by raising his knee sharply against it. Hacking was permissible and, as there were no umpires to appeal to in the case of a breach of the rules, such as, for example, off-side play, the innocent party used to take the law into his own hands, and with a shout of 'Off-side, Sir,' administer the orthodox punishment by violently kicking the shins of the offender.

Hacking or tripping over were quite as much resorted to as tackling, and though they may in these more civilised days appear a rather brutal and crude method of stopping a runner, they required for success the greatest skill and accuracy ... And not only was it legal to hack over the carrier of the ball, but also the first on side, and I have seen as many as four of the van brought to earth by this means.[14]

Stonyhurst: Catholic families in England, after the Reformation, sent their sons to English schools on the Continent. Three of these later became Downside, Ampleforth and Douai. Another was started by Jesuits at St Omer(s) in Artois, then in the Spanish Netherlands. Later Artois was ceded to France, and in 1750 'The College obtained from Louis XV the coveted title of 'Collège Royal' ... There were ninepins and trap, bat and ball; but besides these there was undoubtedly football for we find it described in some Latin verses as the pursuit of the 'windy ball'.

> *Tum poterant iuvenes rapido vacua atria circum,*
> *Cursu ventosas exagitare pilas.*

In 1762 the destruction of the Society of Jesus in France forced the school to move to Bruges in Flanders, and later to the Prince-Bishopric of Liège. Vicomte Walsh in his *Souvenirs de Collège* tells us that the boys were playing a match when the news came of the execution of Louis XVI. He says: *'Nous étions donc fort animés à une partie de football (ballon lancé avec le pied.)'* [15] In 1794 the approach of the Revolutionary armies threatened, and the school escaped to England to the Lancashire mansion of one of its alumni at Stonyhurst.

Charterhouse: A player was off his side, unless he had at least 3 opponents between him and the other goal.

Eton: In the Field game the ball, which is round and about half the size of an Association ball, may never be handled. Progress is made altogether by dribbling and by charging under the kicks of the behinds, and so preventing the opposite behinds from returning the ball effectively. It is therefore a virtue in a behind to kick high as well as far, so that his forwards may have time to reach the spot where the ball will fall ... if the mass of his own side charge together under the ball they are none of them sneaking [offside] ... it involves a continued pursuit of the ball.[16]

St Peter's, York: Printed rules of the game as played at the school existed in 1856 and these rules were revised in 1873. In both sets of rules there is a rule against standing on the goal bar to intercept the ball. Three centuries earlier, in 1566, it was charged against Christopher Dobson and other boys that 'they plaied at the foote ball within the Cathedrall Churche of York'. They confessed that Dobson 'brought it in and ther was but one stroke'. The sentence was that Dobson should be put in the stocks and have 'sex yerkes with a birchen rod upon his buttocks'.[17]

Shrewsbury: The recognised punishment in early days for 'cutting' dowling was a kicking. In 1870 a day-boy brought an action for assault against the captain of Day-boys F.C. The magistrates dismissed the case. From the pre-1866 rules of the Shrewsbury School Foot Ball Club: 'When the ball is kicked beyond the limits of the side boundary lines, the first player who touches it shall throw in from the point on the boundary lines it left the ground, in a direction at right angles with the boundary line'. This origin of the words touch and touch-line is repeated in other contemporary rules.

Rugby: A letter from Judge Thomas Hughes to the Sub-Committee of the Old Rugbeian Society looking into the Origin of Rugby Football 1897: ... In my first year, 1834, running with the ball to get a try by touching down within goal was not absolutely forbidden, but a jury of Rugby boys of that day would almost certainly have found a verdict of 'justifiable homicide' if a boy had been killed in running in. The practice grew, and was tolerated more and more, and indeed became rather popular in 1838-39 from the prowess of Jem Mackie, the great 'runner in' ... The question remained debatable when I was Captain of Big Side in 1841-42 when we settled it (as we believed) for all time. 'Running-in' was made lawful with these limitations, that the ball

60a. The kick off. The three trees infringing on the pitch were used tactically by the players.

60b. Touch. First illustration of a line-out.

60c. Scrummages were
upright and the ball was
worked out by hacking.

60d. The place-kick. The
players on the right are
waiting to charge as soon as
the ball touches the ground.

60e. The Origin of the Try.
When one of the small boys
defending the goal touched the
ball down behind the goal-line
he had the right to punt it out.
When an attacker touched
down he stayed behind the
line and gently punted the ball
into the hands of one of his
own side standing just over
the line. The latter, having
made a fair catch, could make
his mark. This allowed him to
retreat as far as was needed
for a try at goal by place-kick.
In 1883-4 this intermediate
stage was eliminated in favour
of the present system.
'Scoring in the early days was
by means of goals only. Big

must be caught on the bound, that the catcher was not 'off his side', that there should be no 'handing on', but the catcher must carry the ball in and 'touch down'. Picking up off the ground was made absolutely illegal ...

The ground [in 1871] included a flagstaff, a walnut-tree, an ash-tree; a row of full-grown elms, and a clump of three more elms known as the 'three trees', and also one of the posts, and part of the cross-bar of an old goal, known as 'Case's Gallows, the other part had long been, before my time, the branch of an elm. The 'three trees' formed a marked feature of the game ... Many a time has a side come up after a drop kick, while the ball has been falling slowly and jerkily down from the branch. Alas! two of them are gone, and one alone remains on the new touch-line, a shadow of their former greatness.[18]

Christ's Hospital: Football matches were played before breakfast for no other reason than that the wearing of jerseys instead of the cumbersome long blue coats was then alone permitted. Collaring or rather tackling low, as practised without much risk on grass, would have spelt murder on asphalt so that the custom was to tackle high. So inveterate became this habit, that it survived among a later generation of Old Blues, to the amazement of the clubs they played.[19]

Repton: From its 1862 Football Rules: Shouts of disparagement, loud chaffing, and clapping or other expressions of satisfaction at the failure of antagonists, are entirely opposed to the spirit of the game and to an honourable feeling of rivalry; and the leaders of a side are to put down such conduct on the part of their followers at all hazards.

Manchester Grammar School: In the 1870s, it is said, one of our boys was asked the following question: 'What games do you play at The Manchester Grammar School?' 'Games!' was the astonished reply. Then with a wealth of scorn, 'We don't play GAMES at The Manchester Grammar School!'[20]

Winchester – GOAL. The arrangement, which survived till about 1845, by which the functions of goal, goal-keeper and umpire were assigned to one individual.[21] 'He stood with his legs wide apart, and a gown rolled up at each foot: if the ball was kicked directly over his head or between his legs, without touching it, it was a "Goal" and scored three for the party which kicked it; if directly over one of the gowns at his feet, a "Gowner", which counted two; or if it passed between either of the gowns and the last boy of the line on that side, a "Schitt", one.'[22]

Interschool Matches

In the late 1850s the first reports of inter-school matches appeared in the press. In 1858 in Edinburgh Merchiston Castle drew with the Royal High School. 'The Rugby School game had just been introduced into Merchiston and they "did not fully understand all the rather complex rules".'[23] Later the same year Merchiston drew away at Edinburgh Academy. This match is still played annually, probably the oldest continuous football fixture anywhere. In England the first reported matches were Lancing v. Brighton (0-1) and Westminster v.

Side Matches continued for three, five or seven afternoons, or until three goals had been scored. If no goal had been kicked after three days a match would be abandoned. At the end of these titanic struggles no one was content with a draw ... 'Up to 1875 a match could not be won unless a goal had been scored. It was then decided that if no goal had been kicked, or the score was equal a match could be decided by a majority of tries, but that a single goal should count more than any number of tries. 'Cheltenham College was the first to work out a system to quantify the advantages in play ... The scheme of points developed at Cheltenham was adopted by the R.F.U. in 1886, allowing three points for a goal and one for a try, though the try was discounted if it was converted.' Jennifer Macrory (1991), late Archivist Rugby School, *Running with the Ball*

61. Edinburgh Academy (founded 1824) c.1830. In 1858 Merchiston Castle played football against the Royal High School and Edinburgh Academy, according to the rules of Rugby School. These matches in Edinburgh were the first Rugby Football matches in Scotland, and were probably the first school football matches anywhere. Hoops still popular in 1830.

Harrow (1-0) in December 1860. In 1858 an Eleven which included eight Harrovians had played Westminster, and next year Westminster had drawn against an Old and Present Harrow XIV which included just one Old Harrovian, a match they found frustrating: 'The game of each is in so many parts totally different from that of the other.'

In the early years of interschool matches teams sometimes included one or two Old Boys or masters, which confuses the issue in determining the first school matches. Westminster and Harrow were certainly the trail-blazers. In 1861 at Vincent Square Westminster welcomed Harrow again (1-1), and Eton (0-2). Also in London Wimbledon School drew with Kensington G.S. on Wimbledon Common (0-0). In 1862 the two Bedford schools met, and in 1863 Westminster played Charterhouse for the first time in what remains the oldest continuous football fixture in England. In 1864 Highgate and Merchant Taylors', Forest and KCS, Bradfield and Radley, and Marlborough and Clifton competed. This last game was the first inter-school rugby match (based on Rugby School rules) played between two English schools, 20-a-side. Like the Bradfield and Radley match, different interpretation of the rules led to a break in the fixture.

For many years no regular foreign matches were played except against Old Marlburians, though occasionally the School tried conclusions with teams of Old Rugbeians or the Blackheath Club. No inter-school game was attempted till 1864, when a match was arranged with Clifton College: but the event was attended with such unhappy consequences that the experiment was not again repeated for nearly thirty years.

In this year of grace the Captain of the Twenty was J.A. Boyle. He was a fast runner, a sure place-kicker, and a brilliant 'drop'. He had, when running, a curious and remarkable knack of holding the ball by one hand at the apex in a kind of clawlike clutch, and of using it thus grasped as a weapon of defence against being collared, and when about to drop he would balance it for the moment in his extended palm.

The match was played with twenty-a-side at Marlborough, and it had been arranged that, in accordance with the home rule, hacking should be barred, though the Clifton regulations permitted it. Marlborough who possessed considerably the stronger team, kept the game well in their opponents' goal from the start and got several touchdowns, none of which, however, was turned into a goal. [i.e. no points.]

Now whether it was that agreement as to no hacking over was misunderstood, or that the Clifton Twenty became irritated at being presssed, is not clear: but this is certain, that before long cries broke from the Cliftonian throats of 'Hack him over!' 'Hack him!' whenever a run was attempted on the part of Marlborough. These suggestions were soon put into practice, and naturally provoked reprisals. A great

62. Clifton 'Caps' in 1865. C.B.L. Tylecote (left) was full-back in the historic 1864 match at Marlborough.

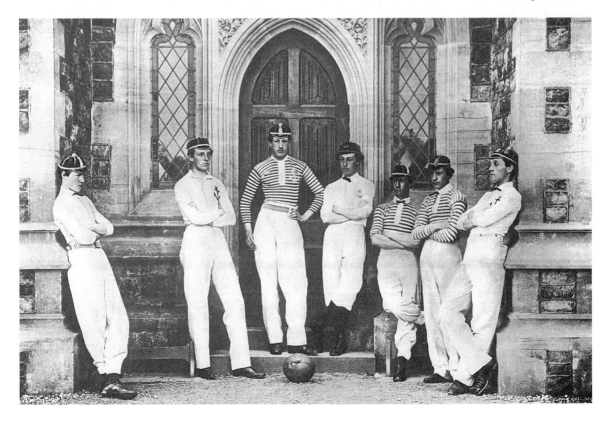

deal of hot blood was engendered, and at one time it looked very much as if the match would degenerate into a free fight.

At this juncture Boyle walked up to the Master [Dr G.G. Bradley] who was standing at the touch-line looking on. 'I think we'd better stop the game, sir, hadn't we?' 'No, no!' came the clear, decisive reply, 'They'll think we're afraid of them. Win the game first, and then talk about stopping if you like!' Boyle strode back to his place behind the squash with determination in his heart. His chance was not long in coming. A few minutes afterwards he got hold of the ball and started for a run. Twice he was brought to the ground by an insidious hack, and twice he struggled to his feet still clutching the ball in his curious grasp. A moment more, and he had by a brilliant drop, executed just in the nick of time, sent the ball flying plump and fair between the Clifton goal-posts as for the third time he was rolled over on the grass: and at the sight there burst forth such a cheer from Marlburian throats as has never before nor since been heard on the football field. Marlborough honour was satisfied, and the pent-up enthusiasm of the School knew no bounds.

The opposing hosts, after the call of 'No game', found time to smooth their ruffled feelings, and parted in the end on amicable terms: but the traditions and legends of the match lasted on for many years, and the experiences of the day led to the effectual discouragement of further contests with any alien team for some time. A.G. Bradley, A.C. Champneys and J.N. Baines (1923), *A History of Marlborough College*

Prior to all these matches, in 1857, Westminster had met the East India College, Haileybury at Vincent Square in bizarre circumstances. The College had been established to train the servants of the East India Company in India, and the match was played on the day after it had effectively ceased to exist. 1857, the year of the Sepoy Mutiny, also saw the end of the Company in India and of the College.

During the greater part of yesterday the metropolis was enveloped in a dense fog, to the great inconvenience of business and public traffic. In the northern districts almost total darkness prevailed ... The fog penetrated into the House of Commons ... Hon. Members were seen flitting about as through a mist, and it was with difficulty that any prominent characters could be recognised ... On the river all navigation was suspended ... whilst in the much-frequented thorough-fares omnibus and cab travelling proved exceedingly dangerous ... *Daily Telegraph* (9 December 1857)

'The game was played in dense fog and the result was never decided'.[24] As the young men of the East India College were nineteen at the youngest, it is a pity that this strange encounter cannot perhaps be classified as the first school football match. Haileybury took over the premises of the East India College, when it was founded in 1862.

Association Football

Before these matches there was no pressure on schools to conform to a unified set of rules; but in 1863 a series of articles by John D. Cartwright in the *Sporting Gazette* 'advocated representatives of schools and universities meeting, to draw up a set of laws for universal adoption ... A meeting took place; but it was found that men were fast wedded to their several systems, and refused to relinquish them or amalgamate with others. Eton thought the Rugby game plebeian, Rugby dubbed the Etonians cowards for not approving of "hacking".'[25] There was no prospect of unification through the schools. Instead it was the continuing interest of their Old Boys in the game they had played at school and their desire for a common code of laws that eventually brought about not unity, but duality.

In October 1863, under the Presidency of Mr A. Pember of the No Names (Kilburn) Club, representatives of a number of metropolitan clubs, meeting at the Freemasons' Tavern, Great Queen Street, Lincoln's Inn Fields, formed themselves into the 'Football Association' with the express purpose of drawing up a code of rules for universal adoption. The majority being 'old public-school men of fame', they were anxious for the support of the leading schools, although they did not expect them to give up their traditional games altogether. The Association's first Secretary, Mr E.C. Morley of the Barnes Club, invited the football captains to the next meeting in London 'declaring that their opinions and advice would be beneficial in helping to draw up the rules'.

Westminster wrote to decline. Harrow's captain, C.G. Browne, replied asking 'for further particulars as to the objects of the Football Association, and the advantages to be gained from joining it ... The head master directs me to say that under no circumstances could he allow the representative of Harrow to attend the annual meeting if such meeting were held during the Harrow School term'. Morley wrote again and received the reply. 'At present Harrow is not willing

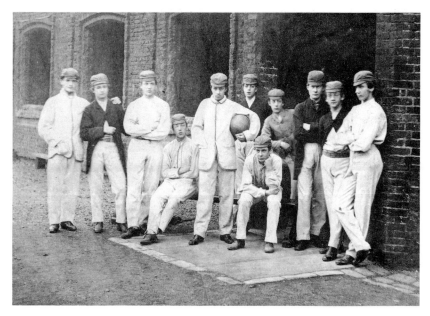

63. The Charterhouse Football XI of 1863 outside the Cloister. The Captain, B.F.Hartshorne (with the ball) was the only representative of a Public School to attend the second meeting of the Football Association at the Freemasons Tavern, Great Queen Street, Lincoln's Inn Fields. He had a little over a mile to travel from the school.

to join the Football Association. We cling to our present rules, and should be very sorry to alter them in any respect. Therefore we will remain at present as lookers on till we can judge what appears best to be done'. Rugby, Eton and Winchester did not even reply. The Charterhouse captain, B.F. Hartshorne, did attend the meeting, (he had a little over a mile to travel), but eventually felt unable to join the Association in isolation from the other public schools. Shrewsbury, approached a little later, also declined.

At a stormy meeting later in the same year the Association's rules were drawn up to exclude running with the ball and hacking. These were the intractable points at issue on which the decisive break was made. Blackheath, an influential club established by some Old Rugbeians, resigned from the F.A. taking some of the membership with them. Their representative protested: 'If you do away with it [hacking, holding, tripping], you will do away with all the courage and pluck of the game, and I will be bound to bring over a lot of Frenchmen who would beat you with a week's practice'. There followed a period of crisis for the fledgling Association. 'Notwithstanding all efforts ... the movement did not progress, and at the commencement of the season 1866-7 three years after its foundation only the following ten clubs were members:

> Barnes F.C.,
> Civil Service F.C.,
> Crystal Palace F.C.,
> Kensington School F.C.,
> London Scottish (Rifles) F.C.,
> No Names (Kilburn) F.C.,
> Royal Engineers (Chatham) F.C.,
> Sheffield F.C.,
> Wanderers F.C.,
> Worlabye House (Baty's) F.C.[26]

In 1867, however, when these ten surviving clubs had had experience of playing each other and several rules had been amended, including the strict offside rule to approximate with the more liberal Charterhouse and Westminster practice, the new Secretary, R.G. Graham, (quoted above), wrote to every known football club in the United Kingdom, inviting membership. 'The response was gratifying, particularly in the adhesion of the two important public schools, Westminster and Charterhouse.' The number of clubs trebled to thirty. These included Forest School, which later had the distinction of becoming the only school ever to play in the F.A. Cup (started in 1872);[27] but not yet any future member of the Football League, founded in 1888. At the subsequent meeting letters of regret were read out.

Mr J. R. Sturgis, writing from *Eton College*, said he had given the

64. Uppingham Football XV 1876/7 in front of its 40 foot wide 7 foot high goal. At Borth (Cardiganshire) where the school had moved temporarily to avoid the typhoid epidemic in Uppingham.

proposal that Eton should join the Association every consideration, but had come to the conclusion that the rules, though unobjectionable in themselves, were too lax and simple. They were, however, so similar to the Eton rules, that they could undertake to play them if necessity required. [The Old Etonians won the F.A. Cup in 1879 and 1882.] He thought their rules involved so much more science and honest work, that he hoped he should never see any game but the Eton game played there. He concluded by saying he thought the Association a capital institution, and one which tended to increase the importance of football, yet he thought it for the interest of the game to preserve the varied forms of it which existed in the public schools.

Mr Edward S. Roscoe, writing from *Radley College*, regretted they could not join, though he wished sincerely all schools would play the same rules. He concluded by saying if Eton, Harrow, and Rugby would give up their separate rules, other schools might be induced to follow their example. Mr F. Ellis from *Rugby* declined, owing to the Association rules differing so thoroughly from theirs. He wished, however, a code of rules could be drawn up which might be used by all playing the Rugby game. He concluded with 'If the Football Association wish to complete thoroughly their good work, they might turn their attention to this subject'. The Association, however, had its hands quite full ...[28]

Some thirty years later Graham wrote in an article on 'The Early History of the Football Association', appearing in *The Badminton Magazine of Sports and Pastimes* 1899:

The fact of two schools, Westminster and Charterhouse, having joined, whilst so many late members of other schools, amongst them the late captains of Eton and Radley Football Clubs, and the Rev. C. Thring of Uppingham [the Headmaster's brother and a prime mover in promoting universal rules], writing, heartily approving of the adoption of the code of rules, gave great impetus to the movement.

Rugby Football

Eight years after the birth of the Football Association, the Rugby Football Union was founded in London in 1871 by those clubs which rejected the Association's rules. Two of the twenty original members were St Paul's School and Wellington College. In framing the new laws the clubs were again in disagreement over hacking. Ironically, it was the Blackheath representative who persuaded the others to outlaw it. The Union made rapid progress, Tonbridge, Dulwich, King's (Canterbury), Sherborne, Epsom, Marlborough and many other schools and clubs affiliating to it. For a number of years some clubs played to the new Union rules, while a minority remained faithful to those of Rugby, until the school accepted the Union's Fifteen game in 1876, adopted R.F.U. rules in 1881, and formally joined the Union in 1890.

In contrast to the Rugby Football Union's later and successful formation in 1871, the years following the birth of the Football Association in 1863 were very difficult ones. Apart from the schools, none of which joined the Association, there was no wide background of football practice and competition. In his 1899 article R.G. Graham, who was appointed Honorary Secretary of the F.A. in 1867, wrote: 'Few have any idea of the struggles against prejudice and even ridicule, which the small body which formulated and worked at the idea had to contend with, to enable football to become a national game.' The following extracts give reason to his complaint.

The Position of 'Soccer'

To be superior in Rowing should ever be the aim of every Englishman, as the main is peculiarly our own; all other nations having, since the times of the Spanish Armada and its disgraceful defeat, owned our supremacy at sea. It tends to enlarge and strengthen the numerous muscles in the arms, and gives additional vigour to the whole frame ... Cricket – the most scientific, diversified and noble of English games, and the prince of all pastimes, of all climes, in all ages – does much towards the formation of a healthy and robust constitution and frame ... Cricket has always been popular; but never more so than at the present time when private speculators pay down incredible sums to entice good cricketers over into our colonies. Wynne Edwin Baxter (1863), 'The Utility of Athletic Exercises' in *Routledge's Every Boy's Annual*

Football does not even feature in this article.

There were only six gentlemen present, Sheffield being represented by

Mr W. Chesterman. Mr Morley* said he was a little discouraged at the paucity of attendance at the meeting, when he remembered that at the commencement of the association in 1863 they had a crowded room, and much more enthusiasm was displayed by those who attended in the interest of the pleasant pastime of football than had ever been shown since ... He confessed he should like to see more clubs represented at the meeting ... He thought they should seriously consider that night whether it were worth while to continue the association or dissolve it; if after discussion they considered they had made the rules perfect, what was the utility of meeting again to do nothing? They had devoted time, patience and trouble to give these rules to the public,and he thought the public should now go on by themselves until another association was requisite. *Bell's Life in London*

From apathy to ridicule:

... the good old and essentially English game of Football, which among the boys of our public schools paves the way, as it were, and prepares them for many another hard fight which in due time they have to encounter in the world ... I have added the rules drawn out by the Football Association, a band of antagonistic brethren who met together in London and attempted a compromise, but from whose efforts not much good has hitherto sprung. Lovers of football are the most conservative people in the world, and real lovers of Football are necessarily a little bigoted when reform is concerned. George Routledge (1867), *Handbook of Football*

By 1868 things were looking up a little.

And there are other sports which are not dead or dying, which are fine and noble in their way, and as to which we feel that we shall be open to reproach from their lovers in that we have omitted them; but, good as they are, we have not thought them to be of sufficient general interest to warrant us in classing them with the great British Games. Of these Foot-ball may perhaps stand first. Foot-ball in latter days has been making a name for itself, and has been becoming famous by the strength of its own irregularity and lawlessness. Because it is without an acknowledged code, the disciples of this and that school of players have been enthusiastic and eloquent. We by no means grudge Foot-ball the name it has won for itself; – but it has hardly as yet worked its way up to a dignity equal with that of Hunting and Shooting, or even with that of Cricket and Boat-racing. *British Sports & Pastimes*, Ed. Anthony Trollope

One of Graham's successors as Honorary Secretary of the Football Association was C.W. Alcock (1870-95). In 1872, in imitation of the Cock House knock-out competition he had experienced at Harrow, he invented the F.A. Cup. Another imaginative move was to publish a *Football Annual*. By publishing details of all clubs which responded

---

* Mr E.C. Morley of the Barnes Club, the F.A.'s first Hon. Secretary from 1863-6, then its President, was in the chair for the Association's A.G.M. at the Freemasons' Tavern in March 1867.

to his invitation, including the code of football they followed, he encouraged matches between them, whether members of his Association or not. This had the effect of publicising football, increasing fixtures, and ultimately helping to produce two universal codes.

The 1873 *Football Annual* lists 193 Metropolitan and Provincial football clubs in England, playing to the following codes:

> 53 Association (including Aldenham, Brentwood, Forest and Lancing)
> 16 Rugby (Blundell's, King's (Rochester), Leeds G.S., Wimbledon).
> 81 Rugby Union (Christ's College (Finchley), Dulwich, Epsom,
>   Highgate, Hurstpierpoint, Kensington G.S., Liverpool, Godolphin,
>   Merchant Taylors', Mill Hill, St Paul's, Sherborne, U.C.S.)
> 22 Sheffield Association
> 1 Derbyshire Association
> 1 Uppingham School
> 4 Rugby without hacking or tripping (City of London, K.C.S.)
> 3 Rugby modified (St Peter's (York), Brighton)
> 4 Association modified
> 1 Modified Association & Cambridge University rules
> 7 Plays both

The *Football Association* had made a fair advance since 1867, but the largest number of Clubs followed *Rugby Union*, which had only been in existence for 2 years. The game developed rapidly in its early years. Teams were reduced from 20 to 15. Head-down scrummaging and heeling, previously regarded as unfair, because the whole scrum became off-side, were accepted. Passing the ball when about to be tackled, instead of putting it down at once, was legitimised. All this made for a more open game.

The Sheffield Association: Its rules differed from those of the London-based Football Association, but like them were an amalgam of Public Schools' rules.[29] Matches between Sheffield and London Associations (and between County Associations) led to common amended rules (no handling; corners), development of tactics (passing and heading, first practised in Scotland and the North), and Sheffield's adoption of all London's rules in 1877.

The Derbyshire Association followed Sheffield rules. Organisation of the game initially was by County or District Associations. All of them came into line with London during the 1870s.

The Scottish F.A., founded 1873, agreed rules with the Football Association in 1882, but the two Associations remain separate, as do the Welsh and Northern Ireland Associations.

Uppingham Rules were introduced by the headmaster, Edward Thring (1853-87), and were modified by his brother, Charles, an

1 When formed
2 Number of members
3 Club ground, where situated
4 Distance from station and name of station
5 Dressing-room where situated
6 Rules whether Association, Rugby or Rugby Union
7 Name & Address of Secretary or Managing Officer
8 Colours
9 Results of Matches
10 Results of Goals

7. W. B. Wilson, 85, Northbrook Street Newbury.
8. Blue.
9. Won 1, lost 4, drawn 2.

Northampton.

1. 1874.
2. 40.
3. Race Course.
4. One mile from Midland; one-and-a-quarter miles each from L. and N.W., and Market Harborough Line.
5. Close to the ground.
6. Rugby Union.
7. J. C. Wills, Hon. Sec., 49, Regent Street.
8. Scarlet and black.
9. Played 3, won 2, drawn 1
10. Won 2, lost 0.

Norwich.

1. 1868.
2. 60.
3. Newmarket Road, Norwich.
4. One-and-a-half miles from Thorpe, and three-quarters-of-a-mile from Victoria Station, G.E.R.
5. On the ground.
6. Rugby Union.
7. L. Prior, the Close, Norwich.
8. Violet and black jersey and stockings, white knickerbockers, violet black and yellow cap and tassel.
9. Played 11, won 5, lost 1, drawn in favour 2, drawn against 1, ties 2.

Nottingham Forest

1. 1865.
2. 110.
3. Nottingham Forest.
4. A mile and a half from Nottingham Station, M.R.
6. Association.
7. W. R. Lymbery, 5, Tennyson Street, Nottingham.
8. Scarlet.
9. Won 8, drawn 5, lost 4.
10. Won 19, lost 22.

Notttingham Law.

1. 1869.
2. 50.
3. Nottingham Meadows Cricket Ground.
4. Quarter-of-a-mile from Nottingham Station.
5. On the ground.
6. Association.
7. Fred. Marriott, 25, Castle Terrace, Nottingham.
8. White and blue stripes.
9. Played 9, won 1, lost 4, drawn 4.
10. Won 1, lost 3, drawn 5.

Panthers.

1. 1873.
2. 85.
3. Sturminster Market.
4. Close to Bailey Gate Station.
5. Sturminster Market Inn.
6. Association.
7. E. G. Farquharson, Hinah House, Blandford, Dorset.
8. Brown and yellow.
9. Played 5, lost 1.

Preston Grasshoppers.

1. 1869.
2. 48.
3. Preston Cricket Ground.
4. Half mile from Preston Station.
5. Pavillion on the ground.
6. Rugby Union.
7. Geo. H. Dickson, West Cliff, Preston.
8. Blue and white stripes.
9. Won 4, lost 5.

Radley College.

2. 100.
3. The School Ground.
4. Half mile from Radley Station.
5. At the College.
6. Nearly Association.
7. The Captain of Football, Radley College, Abingdon.
8. Cherry and white.
9. Played 9, won 1, lost 3, drawn 5.

Reading.

1. 1871.
2. 85.
3. Reading Recreation Ground.
4. Three hundred yards from Reading Station.
5. The "Queen," Reading.
6. Association.
7. J. E. Sydenham, Reading.
8. Dark blue and white stripes.
9. Played 10, won 4, lost 1, drawn 5,
10. Won 14, lost 7.

Reading Hornets.

1. 1873.
2. 50.
3. Reading Recreation Ground.
4. Close to Reading Station.
5. The "Upper Ship Hotel."
6. Association.
7. G. Gibson, King's Road, Reading.
8. Amber and black jersey and stockings, black velvet cap with gold tassel.

Reading School.

1. 1872.
2. 240.
3. The School Ground.
4. Half-mile from Reading Station.
5. The School House.
6. Rugby Union.
7. R. S. Hedley, the School, Reading.
8. Blue and white.

Reigate Priory.

1. 1870.
2. 36.
3. Cricket Ground.
4. Quarter of mile from Station.
5. On the Ground.
6. Association.
7. L. Chave, The Hermitage, Church Street.
8. Dark blue cap, stockings, white jersey.
9. Won 2, lost 10, drawn 8.
10. Goals for 19, against 29.

Rochdale Athletic.

1. 1871.
2. 120.
3. Belfield, Rochdale.
4. Quarter-of-a-mile from Rochdale Station.
5. On the ground.
6. Rugby Union.
7. Jas. Healy, The Butts, Rochdale; H. Lord, 20, Whitworth Road, Rochdale.
8. Crimson and black.
9. Played 15, won 13, lost 2.
10. Won 5, lost 2.

Rochdale Hornets.

1. 1871.
2. 144.
3. Rochdale Cricket Ground, Milnrow Road.
4. Quarter-of-a-mile from Rochdale Station.
5. On the Ground
6. Rugby Union.
7. Alfred Taylor, Egerton Terrace, and A. Irving, East Street.
8. Black and amber.
9. Played 15, won 11, lost 4.
10. Won 6 and 1 poster, lost 2.
11. Won 29, lost 6.

Rochester.

1. 1868.
2. 40.
3. Borstal Road.
4. One mile from Rochester Bridge Station, L.C. and D.R.

65. C. W. Alcock *Football Annual*, 1874. Oxford colleges had adopted Association rules and despite Radley's claim, after changes in their rules, to play 'Nearly Association', the Oxonians were unused to the strict offside. A letter to the *Radleian*: 'We fail to see how the Twelve can be expected to win when half of their opponents deliberately wait in their wrong ground until the ball is kicked to them.' In 1881 because of the difficulty in finding opponents, Radley changed to Association, but not without regrets. Another letter: 'I completely deny that our rules are one atom inferior not only to Association, but to any rules on record.'

Assistant Master at Uppingham 1859-64. In 1862 Charles published his own set of rules ('The Simplest Game') which resembled and anticipated Association. He was an ardent protagonist of a universal code, and on his own initiative, and within a month of its foundation in 1863, he applied for Uppingham to join the Football Association. His brother, though a supporter of games, did not want to give them undue prominence by playing foreign matches, and he caused the application to be withdrawn. The brothers quarrelled and Charles left the school. The Uppingham game, with its 40 foot wide goal, continued throughout Edward Thring's long headmastership. The Uppingham School entry in the 1873 Annual represents not the school, but Kettering, the neighbouring club founded the previous year. Three months before he died, Edward Thring wrote in his diary: 'The football question has come up again. The boys mean to go in for that disgusting game Rugby Union which violates the first principles of every game – to make skill everything and minimise brute force.' Thring's successor, The Rev Dr E.C. Selwyn (1888-1907), within months of his arrival announced the change to rugger. It may be more than a coincidence that, twenty-five years later, his son, the Rev. E.G.Selwyn, made exactly the same announcement within months of his arrival as Warden of Radley (1913-18).

Cambridge Code. At Cambridge in 1863 representatives of Shrewsbury, Eton, Rugby, Harrow, Marlborough and Westminster agreed a Cambridge Code and a few experimental games were played. The F.A. in London made these rules the basis of their own 1863 rules. Earlier at Cambridge, in 1846, a football club had been started whose 1848 code was called the Cambridge Rules, but the game did not last long. (Hockey was then more popular.) One of the small group of founders was – Charles Thring.

The great surge of interest in football in the 1860s and 1870s had not a little to do with the publication of *Tom Brown's Schooldays* by Thomas Hughes. Appearing in 1857 it was tremendously popular, going through five editions in that year alone. It had enormous influence in this period. Remarks such as: ' "I know I'd sooner win two school-house matches running than get the Balliol Scholarship any day" – (frantic cheers)' helped to promote the cult of games – football especially – at schools and elsewhere, as well as erroneously saddling Judge Hughes's headmaster, Dr Arnold, with the reputation of having invented organised games at public schools.

This surge of interest in football was no longer restricted to the public schools and universities. It encompassed a vast new area of national life. The mid-century Factory Acts which for the first time gave Saturday afternoon leisure to industrial workers; the enthusiasm of public school and university men and others to spread knowledge of their game; and the desire of church, chapel and social organisations to provide alternative recreation to the public house by

THE HON: A: F: KINNAIRD:

CAPTAIN OF THE "OLD ETONIANS"

THE ENCLOSURE

S: A: WARBURTON.

CAPTAIN OF THE BLACKBURN OLYMPIC

CROSSLEY KICKING THE DECISIVE GOAL.

THE PRESIDENT PRESENTING THE CUP

GREAT MATCH OF THE SEASON!

ASSOCIATION CHALLENGE CUP. FINAL TIE.

OLD ETONIANS

(HOLDERS)

V.

Blackburn Olympic

WILL BE PLAYED AT

KENNINGTON OVAL

ON

Saturday, March 31st.

KICK OFF · 3·30·

ADMISSION TO GROUND, ONE SHILLING.

To Reserved Inclosure, 1s. extra. Special gate for Reserved Inclosure at Vauxhall side of ground, in front of Crown Baths.

66a, b. The 1883 F.A. Cup Final. The previous year the Old Etonians had beaten Blackburn Rovers in the Final 1-0. Blackburn Olympic beat the holders 2-1 after extra time before 8000 spectators at the Kennington Oval.

67. Old Carthusians v Preston North End in the Quarter-Final of the F.A. Cup 1887. Preston North End won 2-1. The Old Boys of Charterhouse had won the Cup in 1881, beating Old Etonians 3-0 in the Final. Preston beat Wolverhampton Wanderers 3-0 in the 1889 Final. The Preston players are wearing shin-guards. Nottingham Forest claim to be the first to wear shin-guards, invented by their player S.W.Widdowson 1874. Worn outside their stockings, as here. From the mid-90s moved inside stockings. Nottingham Forest also claim priority in playing to a referee's whistle 1878, instead of the handkerchief he used to wave; in staging the first match when a crossbar and net were tried for the first time: North v South 1891; and in being the first club to adopt the formation of 5 forwards, 3 halves and 2 full-backs.

forming local football clubs (Aston Villa, Bolton, Wolverhampton, Everton, Fulham, Southampton etc.) all combined to popularise 'socker'/ 'soccer' for players and spectators alike. In 1883 the world was turned upside down when the Old Etonians, the holders of the F.A. Cup, were defeated in the Final at Kennington Oval by Blackburn Olympic. Comment in the *Eton College Chronicle*, though less than gracious, correctly foreshadowed the way ahead:

> So great was their ambition to wrest the Cup from the holders that they introduced into football a practice which has excited the greatest disapprobation in the South. For three weeks before the final match they went into a strict course of training, spending, so report says, a considerable time at Blackpool, and some days at Bournemouth and Richmond. Though it may seem strange that a football Eleven com-

posed of mill-hands and working men should be able to sacrifice three
weeks to train for one match, and to find the means to do so, yet when
we reflect on the thousands who attend and watch the matches in
Lancashire, and so swell the revenues of the Clubs, and on the enthusiasm of the employers of labour in the pursuits and successes of their
countrymen, it is not so surprising.

Two years later in 1885 professionalism was introduced, and 1888
saw the formation of the Football League by twelve clubs, six from
Lancashire and six from the Midlands.

Football was once more the game of the working-classes, but now
for the first time with universal rules, and under the control of the
Football Association. The Rugby Football Union remained middle-
class and amateur when it refused to recognise broken-time payment
to Yorkshire and Lancashire mill-hands. As a result, in 1895, nearly
all their clubs defected to form the Northern Union (renamed Rugby
League in 1922), which adopted 13 a-side and changed the laws to
encourage open play. League remains localised, but in its heartlands
both Union and Association play second fiddle.

The Seal of Approval

The Clarendon Commissioners' Report on the Public Schools, published in 1864, put the seal of approval on their new attitude towards
team games:

> The cricket and football fields are not merely places of amusement,
> they help to form some of the most valuable social qualities and manly
> virtues, and they hold like the classroom and the boarding house, a
> distinct and important place in public school education ... The impor-
> tance which boys themselves attach to games is somewhat greater

68. A Maul in Goal. Mauls in
goal were abolished in 1893
(see p. 101, re Marlborough).

perhaps than might reasonably be desired, but within moderate limits it is highly useful.

From direct opposition or indifference, to grudging acceptance, to active support, to compulsion – such was the progress of authority's attitude to organised games throughout the 19th century; encouragement and advice – but not direction – in later years being given by masters who at school and university had themselves learned to enjoy these 'manly and muscular diversions'. In the two decades before the First World War 'the cult of athleticism' among boys and masters alike intensified to an exaggerated degree, as can be seen in the emphasis on sport in school magazines of the period.

Outdoor team games and sports of all kinds have been called Britain's gift to the world in the 20th century, (including a universal sporting vocabulary, all the way from 'fairplay' to 'hooligan'). The public schools played a leading role in many of them, pre-eminently in the two codes of football, of the dozen currently played, which have spread all over the world. The palm must go to the boys of the seven old schools in the early years of the 19th century, who succeeded, in the face of strong opposition, in winning acceptance first for team games and then for foreign matches. The Eton and Westminster contests on the Thames will provide further evidence of their endeavours.

69. Winchester Football 1892. Six and Six. The earlier alternative was to play Twenty-two and Twenty-two. Now, as well as Six-a-side it is Fifteen-a-side. The canvas (netting) and side-ropes are integral parts of the game. Said to be the most popular game played at Winchester.

Chapter 6

Boating

The Thames

The impact of the railways in the mid-19th-century virtually put an end to the Upper Thames as a working-river, allowing the new sport of boating to develop unimpeded. For centuries the river had been a main highway for commerce, in heavy bulk cargoes in particular: woodland timber for houses and ships, Oxfordshire building stone, and corn down to London, and imports of sea-coal principally, as well as general cargo, to wharves of riverside towns up to Oxford. London was a great port with ships of many nations providing employment for a huge number of lightermen and other Thames watermen. Under Elizabeth there were said to be 40,000 of them between Windsor and Gravesend. In the 18th century Daniel Defoe counted in the Pool of London 'about 2000 sail of all sorts, not reckoning barges, lighters or pleasure boats, and yachts, but vessels that really go to sea'. Up the Thames a large proportion of the population of riverside towns, such as Marlow, Henley and Abingdon, was dependent for employment on the barge traffic with London.

Navigation on the river could be hazardous. There were many ancient fishing weirs, most of them also acting as mill-dams with mill-pond at one end. The miller made a temporary passage or flash-lock in the weir; the water ponded up behind flooded down, and when levels either side were near equal the barge was flushed through. Cargoes could be swamped in the white water, or the barge might go aground on the shoal formed below each weir by accumulation of silt. To go upstream the crew had to winch the barge up on a windlass situated on the bank, helped by a team of horses on the opposite towing-path. Once through, there could be a wait of many hours before the water level built up again to a navigable depth. For this aid to navigation the miller received a toll from the barge master, who also had to pay riverside landowners for use of the towing-path. Each barge had a sail and sweeps (very long oars) to assist navigation.

Oxford was the head of navigation for larger craft, although smaller boats could reach Lechlade. From Oxford down to Burcot (below Clifton Hampden) was the most difficult stretch of the river, as here the fall in the banks was at its steepest. As barges increased in size, cargoes for Oxford were usually unloaded at Burcot and completed their journey by road. An Act of Parliament under James

70. The Annual Procession of Boats at Eton on June 4th, celebrating the birthday of George
III. Water pageants in England are centuries older than competitive rowing. *The Graphic*, 1870

I appointed Commissioners to improve this stretch, and by 1635 three pound (pond) locks (or 'turnpikes' as they were then more commonly called) were built at Iffley, Sandford, and on the Swift Ditch, the only such 'modern' locks on the Thames until the 1770s. The Swift Ditch is the channel through which the river was temporarily diverted in the 11th century, one mile above Abingdon, to avoid shallows by the Abbey. It rejoins the present course of the river under Culham Bridge. The old channel thus again became the main stream from 1635 until 1790. The stone walls of the lock on the Swift Ditch can still be seen, near the Abingdon Lasher. The channel remains navigable, but now only by canoe.

The Industrial Revolution increased barge traffic enormously. Particularly after the late 18th and early 19th century canals extended the water network and Thames navigation had been improved by the addition of many more pound locks down river. Imports through the port of Bristol, produce of West Country farms, and of Midlands mines and factories reached the Thames Valley and London at under a quarter the cost of road transport by horse-drawn waggon or trains of pack-mules.

> The number of persons required to work the largest barge is six men and one boy [perhaps to lead the towing-horse or to climb the mast as a look-out] ... With stream downwards these barges of 128 tons require only one horse, with which they travel after the rate of three or three and a half miles in the hour; but against the stream in the upward passage from 8 to 14 are necessary, according to circumstances. [Over twice as much freight went downstream as came up, so sometimes a barge would return empty.] Newcastle coal is conveyed upwards as far as Abingdon and Wallingford; but at these places, and at Reading, its consumption is now limited by the Staffordshire coal brought down the Oxford Canal [1790], and by Shropshire and Welch coal brought down the Thames & Severn Canal [1789] ... The exports from the county adjacent to this river consist of corn, wool, timber ... Corn is conveyed principally in its manufactured state, as flour, meal or malt; there being many considerable mills seated on the river, and supplied by its stream. William Mavor (1809), *The Agriculture of Berkshire*

The first half of the 19th century was the period when Thames barge traffic was at its height but by this time the end of the brief Canal Age and to the long story of Thames sailing-barges already loomed large. The Great Western Railway from Paddington reached Reading in 1840, and was open to Bristol in 1841; the Didcot to Oxford line was opened in 1844. Already in 1804, following complaints against bargemen by people using the river for recreation, byelaws were made to control the use of barges. By mid-century the busy river scene would have changed. Although some barge traffic would continue until well into the 20th century, on the Thames, and particularly on the Isis reach, boating for sport and for recreation would have largely replaced it.

Eton and Westminster

Between 1829 and 1847 Eton and Westminster rowed nine long-distance races. These contests of which Eton won five and Westminster four, were held on various stretches of the Thames, and aroused great interest among the public, equal to that shown in the University Boat Race.

At both schools boating records begin in the early years of the 19th century, but boys had 'gone on the water' in the previous century. At Westminster the future Archbishop Markham and the 1st Marquess of Stafford are noted as having been good oars in the 1730s.[1] At Eton in 1797 there were four eight-oared boats and two sixes. 'Eight oars had been manned at Eton before they found their way to Oxford. At Cambridge they appeared still later.'[2] At first these boats were not owned by Eton or Etonians, but were hired from various watermen.

The Watermen and Lightermen's Company was a powerful body in the Pool of London and up and down river. Theirs was a highly skilled job, and a Freeman of the Company would have undergone a seven years' apprenticeship before he was 'free of the river' and able to ply for hire. From 1700 the Company had a virtual monopoly of lighterage and other work on the river. In 1715 their status was reinforced by the London actor-manager Thomas Doggett, who founded Doggett's Coat and Badge, a race for younger watermen, which is still competed for annually, the oldest sculling event in existence. When boats were hired out on the river, they were not entrusted to inexperienced amateur control. At Eton, 'In the early days of the century a waterman stroked and drilled the crews except those of the *Monarch* and the *Dreadnought*.'[3]

Before the 19th century, apart from its main use as conveyance, the chief subsidiary purpose of boating was not for recreation, but for display. Water pageants and processions accompanied by music go back to the 16th century or earlier. In London the elaborate barges of the Lord Mayor and of the livery companies vied with one another in magnificence. At Eton from the last years of the 18th century 'The Fourth of June [George III's birthday] and Election Saturday [when scholars were elected to the school, and from it to Oxford and Cambridge] were celebrated, as in later times, by the Procession of Boats in gala dress; and by fireworks from the Eyot. Each boat previous to 1814 had a fancy dress appropriate to the Boat. After that the crews wore blue jackets with anchors embroidered on the outside arms. In 1828 checked shirts were introduced, and this fashion has continued. On the feast days the boats had tillers fashioned as serpents and garlanded with oak leaves instead of the ordinary wooden tiller or the rudder lines and yokes which they used in the races'.[4]

In 1811 there was a Ten-oar and three boats with eight oars: (1) *Monarch*, ten-oar, (2) *Dreadnought*, (3) *Defiance*, and (4) *Rivals*. Besides these, there were some six-oared boats manned by smaller boys; but with the exception of the Monarch and the Dreadnought each of the

71. Mortar-boards and gowns on the river c. 1850. 'The boat-builders yards were all across the water on the Lambeth side; Searle's yards nearest to Westminster Bridge – here our boats were kept when I was in the eight; Roberts' above that, who found us in boats before Searle; Renshaw's above him, who had the half-deckers; and Noulton and Wyld's above Lambeth Church, who had the best light sculling boats and pair-oars'. *Recollections of a Town Boy at Westminster 1849-1855*

boats had a waterman to pull Stroke, and drill the crew. The practice of having a waterman to each of the Lower Boats continued until 1828, when it was abolished, and, after that, the Captain of each crew rowed the Stroke oar ...

In all the races that were rowed between Sixes or Eights round a turning point there was more or less bumping ... the great point was for the boat, which was left behind at first, to catch its opponent at the turning-point, and then a fight resulted, at the end of which one boat or the other was frequently disabled.[5]

William IV [1830-7] was an ardent patron of the river, and was especially fond of the Fourth of June. One year he gave a dozen dozen of Champagne to be drunk by the boys in the ten-oar but the effect was so disastrous that he was asked to reduce his allowance, and next year he sent only a miserable dozen.[6]

Boating was not formally recognised by the School authorities before 1840, but ever since the beginning of the nineteenth Century boys had been practically free from interference while they were on the river, although the road to it was out of bounds.[7]

In former years considerable difficulty was encountered in getting to and from the Brocas by the necessity of all but the Sixth Form being obliged to shirk [avoid] the Masters, and of all the Lower Boys having to shirk the Sixth Form. However, the river itself was not forbidden; it was simply ignored. On the morning of the 4th of June, 1822, Dr Keate sent for the then Captain of the Boats, and said to him, 'The boys are often very noisy on this evening and late for Lock-up. *You know I know nothing*! But I have heard you are in a position of authority and know a great deal: so I hope you will endeavour not to be late to night, and do your best to prevent disorder'. As it turned out they were not more than an hour late on that day, and there was not quite as much of a row as usual; and, in consequence, Dr Keate expressed his satisfaction, but still professed his ignorance of what had really occurred. None of the Masters went near the river on the 4th of June or Election Saturday, and the fact of Fireworks, and the whole School being late for Lock-up, was winked at on these occasions.[8]

Although Dr Keate affected only to have heard that the Captain of Boats was in a position of authority, an Etonian in Keate's time recalls: '*The* great man, *facile princeps* in the opinion of the school, was the Captain of the boats, and the little fellows looked upon him with awe and generally gave him the credit for being cock of the school also'.[9]

'Boating was forbidden and the Fourth of June was a proscribed day. Keate, however, always had a large dinner party in honour of the anniversary, and announced that lock-up would not be till half-past nine as, on so fine an evening the boys would perhaps like a little extra time in the shooting-fields.'[10] Another Etonian remembers: 'He laughingly said he couldn't see why leave should be extended to ten o'clock, but supposed there was a cricket match or something of that sort going on at that time.'[11]

Keate is known to have interfered in the matter on one occasion only, when, in 1829, he had heard by chance that some of the boats intended to row up to Surly Hall before Easter. He tried to prevent this by threatening to expel any one who should take part in the expedition, but, finding that the boys paid little attention to his threats, he resolved to waylay them and catch them in the act of disobedience. Unfortunately for himself, he made no secret of his purpose, and the boys contrived to hoax him effectually. On the appointed day, a crew of watermen, dressed up to represent Etonians and wearing masks over their faces,started from the Brocas in the *St George*, in the presence of a crowd of boys and townspeople who had come out to see what would happen. Keate caught sight of them from the bank ... and shouted: – 'Foolish boys, I know you all.' 'Lord Alford, I know you.' 'Watt, you had better come ashore.' 'Come here, or you will all be expelled.' The boat, however, pursued its course steadily, several of the Masters giving chase on horseback, and the ruse was not discovered until the crew disembarked and took off their masks with a loud 'hurrah'. Keate was furious, and vowed that he would keep the whole school at Eton two days beyond the time fixed for the beginning of the holidays, unless at least thirty of the boys who had hooted him and other Masters from behind the hedges gave themselves up. As this threat produced no effect, some of the Masters ... asked their respective pupils to say whether or not they had shouted on the Brocas. Eighteen confessed and were accordingly flogged, and twenty-four others who would not incriminate themselves were detained two days ...

The most important result of the affair was that watermen and other 'cads' [boatmen] were thenceforth forbidden to set foot within the wall of the Long Walk at Eton.[12]

In 1840, as a result of a boy's death by drowning, boating was finally recognised, and Etonians were no longer allowed to risk their lives on the river, until after they had passed a swimming test.

The *Westminster School Water-Ledgers* of 1819-20 record

> The Westminsters were this year challenged by the Etonians ... The race [in a six] was at length fixed from Westminster to Kew Bridge against the tide, the Etonians refusing to row back ... The match was put an end to by the positive order of Dr Page.

Page died in 1819, and in 1820 his successor Dr Goodenough followed Page's example. But in the *Eton Boating Book*: 'This year 1820 a challenge was sent from Westminster and accepted but the authorities forbade the match' – threatening to expel anybody who should row. Whichever school made the challenge, neither headmaster was prepared to countenance it. The ban was unpopular. At Eton 'The names of those selected to row, in case the match should have been allowed, were cut in the headmaster's desk in Upper School.'

Nine years later, in 1829, at the beginning of the holidays, the first race did take place, from Putney Bridge through Hammersmith Old Bridge and back. 1829 was also the first year of the University Boat Race – at Henley, and the boat in which Westminster rowed, the *Cam*, was the one in which Cambridge had lost six weeks earlier.

> Curiously enough ... the first Eight that ever went forth from Eton to contest for aquatic honours consisted mainly of boys who were not members of the regular boats. Lord Waterford, Captain of the *Britannia*, had been desirous that one of the boats should be manned by Irishmen, and, on meeting with a refusal from Lord Alford, had seceded with many of his friends. Several of the crews had been reduced, and the Defiance had been abandoned. On the other hand the Irishmen had been going out on the river ... It was Lord Waterford who sent the challenge to Westminster, and it was he who stroked the Etonian crew at Putney. The race was ignored by the Captain of Boats and his supporters.[13]

As with every sporting event of the time, from the 'Fancy' (bare-knuckle boxing) to the 'Turf', from 'Pedestrianism' (professional running) to the 'Canine Fancy' (the public-house rat-pit), 'Aquatics' attracted widespread betting.

> On Monday evening a numerous highly respectable assemblage of amateurs congregated on the river at Putney to witness the contest

between eight young gentlemen of Eton and eight of the Westminster scholars ... Heavy betting took place in favour of the Westminster gentlemen previous to the start, and the interest which this juvenile contest excited among the numerous relatives and friends of the contending parties was, perhaps, never surpassed on any similar occasion. The Etonians and their friends arrived at Putney in a commodious carriage, with four handsome bays; the Westminster scholars in an open barouche with four greys ... It was generally known that Brumwell, of Vauxhall, was to steer the Westminsters; but nearly up to the period of starting, the amateurs were kept in ignorance as to who was to 'take the lines' of the Britannia, and some anxious enquiries were the consequence with those who were desirous of sporting their money, on the result ... The Etonians pulled up to bridge in broad blue-striped Guernsey frocks and dark straw hats, with blue ribbon – true sailor fashion – with the celebrated T. Honey, of Lambeth, as coxswain. This latter circumstance had a material effect on the betting ... The Westminster scholars appeared at the bridge in very neat trim, the whole wearing white shirts and straw hats ... On the signal being given, they went away in style, accompanied along the whole line of the towing-path by between forty and fifty gentlemen on horseback, the majority of whom wore a piece of blue ribbon in a button-hole of their coats. The Westminster gentlemen went ahead at starting by about a boat's length, and continued the lead up the river for nearly half a mile, when the Etonians came opposite their opponents ... and notwithstanding the skill displayed by Brumwell, who nearly succeeded in bringing the nose of his boat on the quarter of that of the opposite party, as she was shooting by, the Eton gentlemen went well ahead, and maintained it throughout the distance, gallantly winning by above a quarter of a mile. *Bell's Life in London*

In 1831 for the second encounter the course was in Eton water, from Maidenhead Bridge to Queen's Eyot below Monkey Island and back. Eton won the 6-mile race, again by a quarter of a mile, in 45 minutes.

Although the Westminster crew were the favourites at ten to one, and said to be 'big enough to eat the Eton boys', they were signally beaten. The anomalous relation then existing between the Masters and the boys is well illustrated by the fact that Keate never heard a word about the race until it was over. The first notice he received of it was at 'six o'clock absence', when, amid loud cheers, 'Bear', a St Bernard dog belonging to one of the masters, Edward Coleridge, was led up to him covered with the pale blue rosettes the boys had worn. He asked the Praepostor by his side what this demonstration meant, and when told:– 'Please, sir, we've just beaten the Westminsters', he smiled, and, as usual, said:– 'Foolish boys!' [14]

The Rev. E. Moore, who had rowed No. 7 in the Eton boat, recalled: 'Within a quarter of an hour of the commencement of 'after twelve', neither an Eton boy nor a horse nor wheels of any sort were visible in either Eton or Windsor, but the Maidenhead road was alive with every possible combination of the three ... the sequel was a solemnly

decorous lecture from the Doctor in 'Keate's Chamber' to the eight. But the Doctor was evidently, nevertheless, well pleased.' [15]

In 1834 the proposed match was from Windsor Bridge to Surly Hall and back; but the King's Scholars were forbidden to row by Dr Williamson, Headmaster of Westminster (1828-46). An attempt to stage the race after the end of term was foiled when he involved the Dean of Christ Church, Oxford and the Master of Trinity, Cambridge. As the Electors to the closed King's Scholarships from Westminster and Eton, they refused to receive anyone in their Colleges if he rowed in the race. *Bell's Life* published a condemnation of the 'Reverend Doctors', and Williamson replied in the next issue. He had told the crew he 'disapproved of such matches, on account of the intemperance and excesses to which both they and I know by experience, they led'. *The School Water Ledger* vilified 'that never to be mentioned, sneaky, spy-retaining, treacherous, cowardly, snivelling, ungentlemanlike, treble damnable shit of a Head Master of Westminster School (merely an M.A.)'.

A third match was permitted in 1836, this time from Staines two miles downstream to Penton Hook and back.

72. The Westminster Eight Winning the Race against Eton in 1845. F.H. Forshall (1884), *Westminster School Past & Present*

The young gentlemen of Westminster came to Staines in a new boat called the *Fairy Queen*, built of fir, expressly for the occasion, by Noulton and Maynard, the well-known watermen, the former taking the lines for his patrons ... Previous to starting, it was agreed upon that no fouling should take place until half a mile of the distance had been rowed. On going away from the bridge the Westminsters went in advance, which position they kept for about a quarter of a mile, Eton pressing them closely. Noulton ... steered the *Fairy Queen* over to the course the Etonians were pursuing and he bored them so closely inshore that ... a foul consequently took place, which lasted five or six minutes, ending in the discomfiture of the *Fairy Queen* who had her rudder struck off, an oar broken, and was turned completely round. The Etonians went away with a cheer, but the Umpires, considering that an infringement of the agreement had taken place, called them back for a fresh start ... The *Fairy Queen* again took the lead, which she held for about three-quarters of a mile, when the Etonians came upon them, and some smart fouling was the result. Eton at length cleared ... In rounding the distance boat they were close together, and immediately after doubling the station punt the Westminsters came alongside and fouled. Eton shortly cleared, but ... the Westminsters caught them on the starboard quarter, which nearly put the *Victory* into the bank stern up. The Etonians ... notwithstanding they were occasionally bumped by the *Fairy Queen* maintained the lead ... winning by several boats' lengths. The match proved a treat throughout, by the spirited and gallant manner in which it was contested by both parties. *Bell's Life*

Next year, 1837, from Datchet Bridge, one-and-a-quarter miles downstream to the New Lock and back, Westminster won for the first time, by 3 to 4 lengths. The previous year both crews had worn blue and white. On this occasion to make a distinction Westminster adopted the pink of their Town Boys, and the victorious boat was also painted pink. 'From that time pink became the recognised colour of the School.'[16]

The tradition of having professional watermen to stroke and steer, even when they no longer owned the boat, ran out of fashion. The stroke disappeared at Eton in 1828, and from this year (1837) professional coxes were dispensed with. The Westminster cox was up to the occasion. 'In turning at the New Lock the Etonians doubled their boat with greater dexterity than their antagonists, and the consequence was that they brought the nose of their cutter bang on to the sixth oar of the Westminsters, who would have shipped some water had not young Lord Somerton bore the *Haidée* up by leaning over on the opposite side.'[17] William Rogers who was in the Eton eight remembers William IV, against doctors' advice, coming down from Windsor Castle 'in a closed carriage, wrapped in a white great-coat, about a hundred and fifty yards from the bridge. As soon as he saw that the Westminsters were ahead, he pulled down the blinds and drove back to the Castle, which I do not think he afterwards left.' The Sailor King died there seven weeks later, as a result, both schools believed, of Eton's defeat. The *Westminster School Water Ledger* reported that after this race: 'Col. Lambert, of the Guards [at Windsor], requested us to dine with the mess which we accepted, and returned through Eton next morning to Town.'

Perhaps it was to prevent such an occurrence that next year, 1838 'The Head-masters of both Eton and Westminster were hostile to the race; and though the Etonians (it being their vacation) were all ready at Westminster Bridge, and the Westminster crew were determined to row, it was prevented at the last hour by Dr Williamson.'

73. *facing page* A bump is made at Shrewsbury c. 1895. At the start on the morrow the third crew will change places with the second. The fourth crew could, in theory, make an overbump on the first and start the next day at the head, but looks more likely to be bumped itself.

74. The Henley Regatta in 1843.

Ashwell Rectory.
August 6th, 1883.
DEAR SIR, – You ask me for some information concerning the stoppage of the race in 1838.

'Infandum … jubes renovare dolorem.'

For no good reason the Head-masters of both Eton and Westminster were averse to the race, and we knew that Williamson would try to stop it, and so we determined to get on the blind side of him. We meant to be very clever, but were in reality convicted of great folly. … We acted on the principle that all is fair in love and war, and, as regards the race, we were at war with Williamson, and felt that any scheme was allowable which would give us the upper hand.

Our artful dodge was to ask for an early play, on the day fixed for the boat race, ostensibly to play a cricket match, and that then the crew – most of whom were engaged in the eleven – should steal off to the river, and row the Etonians. Could any scheme have been more clumsy than this? Was it likely that, when all the world was talking of the boat race, Williamson should be so ignorant of it as to be hoodwinked by our most transparent device? The only result of our scheme was to place ourselves gratuitously in the wrong; to make ourselves obnoxious to the deserved censures of old Westminsters, who are, as a rule, like Brutus, all honorable men, and to make Williamson more determined than ever to stop the race … The only question now for Williamson was how to stop the race? His mere veto would have been of no avail, for the boys were very determined.

No threats of expulsion served to intimidate. They said that, if one was expelled, they would all go. Disobedience to orders, and even mutiny was not far off, for the whole School was proud of its crew, and thought they were going to win. It knew that by strict training and practice every man of it had done his best to deserve success, and it felt that it was a shame that so much self-denial should be sacrificed to a mere whim. But what availed school determination, or school sentiments? The Master ... gave some of the Queen's scholars impositions, so as to keep them in college at the time fixed for the race; but he felt that this measure did not meet the emergency ... No impositions, and no stone walls, would have sufficed to keep those perverse scholars from their thwarts.

... It so happened that there were two fellows in the crew, who had fathers in town. To each of these fathers Williamson went, and said: 'If your son rows, the consequences will be very serious to him.' There is nothing like your vague threat to produce a panic. A very serious consequence smacked of expulsion, and expulsion from a public school at that time implied dis-qualification for the University, and a complete collapse of all professional prospects.

No wonder that the bare hint of such an extreme penalty frightened governors hugely. In this way Hodgson and Pollock, Nos. 5 and 6, were eliminated, and that is how the race was stopped in 1838. Shall I ever forget the horror of that moment, when my father, big brother, and

75. The Henley Regatta in 1844: at the Start.

76. The Henley Regatta in
1844: going down to the Start.

uncle – who was himself one of the masters – broke into my room, and
found me in the very act of donning my white jersey trimmed with
pink? Had they been only a few moments later, I should have been off.
Had I known of their coming, I should have given them the slip. My
father informed me, in the most delicate manner in the world, that I
must not think of rowing. 'I do not agree with Williamson,' he said, 'at
all, but expulsion is a serious thing. You would not be eligible for that
scholarship I mean you to win at Balliol College. You very naturally
deem this race as all-important, but it is insignificant as compared
with your future prospects in life. I am responsible for them, and, sorry
as I am, I must place my decided veto on your rowing.' …

… Alas! for the first and, I trust, the last time in my life, I showed
a disposition to defy paternal authority … It seems so dreadful to be a
deserter, a renegade, or a traitor. I know not what I said, but I
remember very well that the reply of my father was somewhat to this
effect: 'Ah! it is all very well, my fine fellow. I admire your spirit, I feel
very much for your disappointment. But let me tell you this, I am quite
as determined as you are. You will accompany me this moment to
Croydon – there, you need not say nay. Here am I, here is your brother,
and there is your uncle; and, if that is not enough in the way of physical
force, I will call to my aid any requisite number of policemen; so you
had better come at once, quickly.' I was overpowered, but chiefly by
grief, which has not even yet subsided. Thus, malgré moi, was I
dragged away.

It was all in vain for you, Andrewes, to place that written document
in my hand at my exit from Dean's Yard, bidding me to be firm, and
stick to my colors … I was like a calf forced to the sacrificial altar, and

I did feel the next morning the stinging rebuke of our noble captain, my dearest friend, who had actually for the nonce assumed a grim voice, and severe look, as he asked, 'How, Hodgson, could you be so weak?'

... The day before he had chivalrously offered to row the Etonians with two substitutes from the second eight; but this offer their stroke declined, saying, 'If we win, it will be no credit to us, and if we lose it will be a disgrace.'

We felt so sorry for the Etonians; to think that they had brought their boat so far to no purpose, and they seemed such nice fellows. They spoke so kindly, and expressed so much sympathy with us under our humiliating circumstances. The stoppage of that race! Oh, the pity of it! the pity of it! It was a lovely afternoon; the tide was almost slack; there was not a ripple on the surface. I saw, as I passed over Westminster Bridge, the muster of boats on the river, and the surging crowd, which had already gathered on the bridge itself; a crowd doomed, as I knew, to disappointment. No wonder there was indignation! No wonder that Williamson was unblessed that day by those who had been thus causelessly baulked of their sport! No wonder that the journals of the day heaped vituperative epithets on his devoted head, and that the editor of Bell's Life abjured euphemism in his condemnation of the course taken by the Head-master. Many years have passed since then, but not one has produced a day marked in my calendar with so black a cross, or one so fraught with painful remembrance, as that eventful day on which Williamson stopped the race in 1838. It would probably have been a close contest, as both crews furnished afterwards several distinguished oarsmen to the two Universities.

Yours faithfully,
H.W. Hodgson.[18]

Dispensing with professional coxes and the introduction of outriggers in the 1840s led to the end of fouling. The amateur sportsman's view was put by the Umpire after the third University Boat Race in 1839: 'The principles which we always maintained were: first that gentlemen should steer; second (which follows from the first), that fouling should be abolished.' It is ironic to look forward exactly 150 years to the 1989 Boat Race, when professionals were reintroduced as coaches and neither of the steerers was a gentleman. The Umpire on that occasion, Ronnie Howard, had to warn both crews at once as blades clashed, and was quoted as calling it not rowing, but 'confrontation'.

In the 1840s Westminster won three times from Kew Eyot to Putney or from Putney to Mortlake, in 1842, 1845 and 1846. Eton won in 1843 against their 'comparatively diminutive antagonists', [10st 8lb v. 9st 2lb], and in 1847 when 'the Westminsters struggled with the greatest pluck, and their little stroke oar, Barker, astonished the congregated oarsmen by the beauty of his form and the spirit of his rowing'.[19] An Old Westminster records the excitement of victory in 1845:

The race was to be rowed at 2.15, from Barker's rails to Putney Bridge,

77. Cambridge beating Oxford in the Grand with the Umpire's boat in close attendance in 1845.

a course longer by a mile than that used by the Universities in their annual contest. On this occasion I rowed in a light four ... We proceeded up the river till we reached a spot a short distance above Hammersmith Bridge, where we waited to catch the first sight of the contending crews. Far up the reach our view extended for more than a mile. We knew by the time of day that the boats should have left the starting-post a quarter of an hour since. What minutes of throbbing anxiety, as we lay on our oars scanning the water for the first glimpse of them! No sign of them yet! Would they never come?

Suddenly our stroke oar exclaimed with a gasping nervous cry, 'I see the pink oars in the sunlight,' and tremblingly he pointed to where a pinkish mist seemed hovering over the water. A few more seconds and the pink oars were plainly visible, flashing in the light on the river. Then through the still, sultry air came that sound so familiar to frequenters of University boat-races, the huzzas of a distant multitude borne over the water. We began to row out into the river in order to keep some propinquity to the approaching rivals, and in less than five minutes the Westminster Eight was level with us.

In solid form they were rowing, with the well-known long, sweeping stroke. No splash! No hurry! ... Some half-dozen lengths behind came the Watermen's Eight, which should have kept with them to guide and encourage throughout the course. The veteran Noulton held the tiller ropes in the Watermen's boat, and, ashamed of his position astern, was calling out: 'Now, my dear boys, there is no need to row so hard'. Immediately, as if by magic, we, who had just now seemed alone on the river, were surrounded by a miscellaneous fleet of boats. First came steamers staggering beneath their freight of living beings, who sent forth peal after peal of triumphant cheers: 'Rowed, indeed!' 'Bravo,

78. In 1840 it was ruled 'that no boat under any pretence whatever (the umpire excepted) shall accompany the racing boats during the matches'. Breach of rules or artist's licence?

Westminster!' with extraordinary prolongation of the last syllable, as though the shouters feared they might possibly be inaudible ... These and similar shouts resounded from the river and from both banks, on one of which a body of horsemen who had galloped along the towing-path were waving their hats and cheering ...

With the steamers, or immediately in their rear, the eights of the Leander, Thames, Thetis, Neptune, and other clubs came dashing along. Conspicuous among them was the Westminster School second Eight, bearing the flag of the School with the arms and motto, 'In patriam populumque,' gorgeously emblazoned thereon. Intermingled with these, four-oared boats, pair-oared boats, scullers in wherries, randans,[20] muffs in tubs, skilled oarsmen in outriggers, with others for which no name is found, crowded up. In front of all, amid an uproar of applause, and salvos of small cannon from the gardens and hostelries at Putney, the Westminster Eight passed the winning-post. But where was the Eton boat? So far astern that it could not easily be distinguished, amidst the press and crowd of craft on the river.

... The race was won by one minute and five seconds, or about sixty boats' lengths. Then down the river, amidst fresh bursts of cheering from shore and boats. Quickly and lightly we went along, till we reached the landing-place at the Horse Ferry. Up College Street we streamed, with a crowd of navvies and bargees as an escort, who made a tremendous noise, in view of the sixpences to be obtained, and the pots of porter to be drunk at our expense. Presently the stroke of the victorious Eight was hoisted on the shoulders of several big boys and carried round and round Dean's Yard, amidst deafening cheers which became hoarser and hoarser ... What Westminster boy on that night would have exchanged places with the greatest hero of ancient or modern times?[21]

Westminster averaged 9st. 3lb. and Eton 10st. 1 lb.

In this race Westminster had surprised their opponents by appearing in an outrigger against Eton 'in a cutter [inrigged] rather on the antique principle'. Outriggers were invented on the Tyne in 1828. The rowlocks were brought eight inches outside the boat on supports first of wood and later of iron. An oarsman now did not need to be seated up against the far gunwhale in order to exert optimum leverage. Outriggers were not suitable for skilful fouling. 'Inrigged craft glide off each other when gunwhales collide, whereas outriggers foul rowlocks of other boats, and cause delay and even accidents.'[22] So fouling came to an unlamented end. Bumping, its more respectable cousin, survives at Oxford, Cambridge and Shrewsbury (and perhaps elsewhere).

In the 17th and 18th centuries Westminster's scholarship and reputation were second to none. In 1729 numbers had reached a peak of 440, but towards the end of the century decline had begun. Indifferent headmasters, neglect by the Dean and Chapter of the Abbey, a preference for Eton by George III, and the growth of London with the urbanisation of the open fields in the school's immediate surroundings, had all contributed to a spectacular fall in numbers, from 332 in 1819 to a mere 67 in 1841. So Westminster's triple success on the water in the 1840s against Eton's 600 was a real triumph.

In 1851, and again in 1856, permission for a match was refused by successive Westminster headmasters. 'In the fifties Eton rowing had entered upon a very dull and uninteresting phase so far as outside competition was concerned. A few races were rowed against University and College crews, but they evoked little or no interest, as the adversaries were usually more or less scratch crews who were not even in training, though in this respect it is doubtful whether Eton was better off. In 1858, however, there was a welcome change for the better, as Radley challenged Eton and a race came off at Henley.'[23]

In 1860, after a thirteen year break the Eton-Westminster series was resumed. (Could it have been as a result of the success of the Henley occasion? In his speech at the Old Radleian Dinner in 1872, Sewell claimed: 'My correspondence with Eton would show the assistance which Radley gave in restoring matches among Public Schools'.) In each of four races between 1860 and 1864 Eton won easily. Although numbers at Westminster were recovering, they found it difficult to raise a crew of adequate strength and eventually did not issue a challenge. From 1861 Eton had entered at Henley Regatta, which diverted some of her interest. In 1867 at Westminster 'There was no eight, as there were not enough fellows on the water fit to row in one'.[24] Finally the completion of the London Embankment in 1868 made boating very difficult and put a temporary end to Westminster 'Water' until 1872, when a new start was made at a boathouse opposite Hurlingham. But there were no more long-distance matches with Eton. Westminster ceased to row for a second time in 1884 (until 1917). The *Westminster School Water Ledger* reported tersely: 'In 1884, the alteration of hours introduced by the new head-master caused the total discontinuance of boating.' ('... at the unanimous request of the Masters, the Head Master, Dr Rutherford, abolished Water altogether.')[25] The lament in *Blackwood's Magazine* discloses more deep-seated reasons: 'The sewer and the steamboat have strangled one of our nurseries of oarsmen.'

In 1989, to celebrate the 125th anniversary of their last match, river traffic was stopped and Eton and Westminster rowed a light-hearted race between Lambeth and Westminster Bridges, which Westminster is declared to have won.

Henley

The seeds of Henley Regatta were planted in the first race between Oxford and Cambridge, which was rowed over the Henley Reach in 1829. The people of Henley saw the commercial possibilities of an annual regatta. At a public meeting held in the Town Hall in 1839, 'attended by the landed gentry of the neighbourhood and the principal townspeople of Henley-on-Thames', a regatta was established with the primary intention 'of producing most beneficial results to the town', and secondly of being 'a source of amusement and gratification to the neighbourhood, and to the public in general'. An unlimited number of Stewards were elected, who chose from among themselves a Committee to run the Regatta. None of them were rowing men.

From 1839 until 1885 the Old Course started just above Temple Island and finished upstream at Henley Bridge, which served as a convenient grandstand. In the first year the crews had to row under the bridge; but the steps on the Red Lion lawn forty yards below the bridge subsequently became the finishing-line. There were no booms to straighten the course, and the left-hand bend in the last quarter-mile from Poplar Point (near the present finish) up to the bridge gave a big advantage to the Berkshire station. But this was the town's regatta, and the best viewing points for spectators were the bridge and the road between river and Red Lion. Here covered stands were erected for the two days of the Regatta, for the use of the Stewards and 'the élite of Henley'. Everyone was in easy reach of the Red Lion, the Catherine Wheel and the other inns, as well as the shops, and the Town Hall, where the prizes were given out.

When in 1886 the Committee appointed were rowing men, they quickly decided to alter the course. The New Course started below Temple Island and finished at Poplar Point, as it does today. Spectators had to cross the bridge to the public towing-path on the

Berkshire bank, or to occupy boats along the booms, which were introduced to straighten the course. But by then the Regatta was very firmly established, to the town's advantage.

The economic interest of the town in being host to a successful regatta is reflected in a financial report commissioned in 1858 and included in Henley Corporation Minutes. 'The Town was formerly a large corn Market and carried on an extensive trade in the manufacture of Malt and in the carriage of Wood and Merchandize to and from London by the navigation of the River Thames and was the great thoroughfare from London to Oxford and Birmingham, but from the diversion of the thoroughfare by the Great Western Railway and other causes the market has become very small, the malt trade greatly reduced and the Town has become greatly impoverished.' The G.W.R. from Paddington had reached Twyford by 1839. The Didcot to Oxford line opened in 1844. One direct effect was on the Red Lion which had flourished as a coaching-inn. It closed down completely between 1852 and 1859. Another effect was on the river, where horses hauling barges made their laborious way along the towing-path. By 1861 'the navigation was reduced to its lowest point as the Railway and Wickens' waggon perform nearly all the carrying business of the town'. By that time the Twyford-Henley rail link (1857) had replaced the 4-horse-drawn omnibus. But this was to benefit both Town and Regatta.

The 1858 Henley Royal Regatta (It became Royal in 1851 when Albert, the Prince Consort, became its patron, though he was never to visit the Regatta.) took place on Monday and Tuesday, 21 and 22 June. 'As usual the bridge afforded standing room to the carriages of the neighbouring gentry, who can from this point command a view of the whole length of the water by the aid of their glasses, which were called into requisition by the ladies as well as the gentlemen.'[26] 'A commodious stand was erected on the western side of the river, which was well patronised by the nobility and gentry of the neighbourhood, and immediately in front was the splendid band of the Fourth Light Dragoons, in a gaily-dressed vessel which was moored on the Thames.'[27] '... the spaces between racing were relieved by their performances'. There were indeed spaces, as the spectators saw very little racing compared with to-day's Regatta. There were nine events, three of which had a single entrant, who rowed over; and five had but two crews, who contested the final. In the Grand Challenge Cup Cambridge beat Leander in a heat, and then held off London, who as holders had automatically (until 1872) qualified for the Final. Seven races in two days.

Eton and Radley 1858

This match ... we believe had its origin about the time of the University race in which two or three old Radleyans, as well as Etonians were engaged. *Bell's Life*

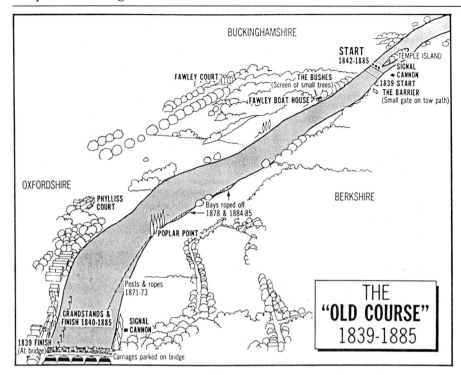

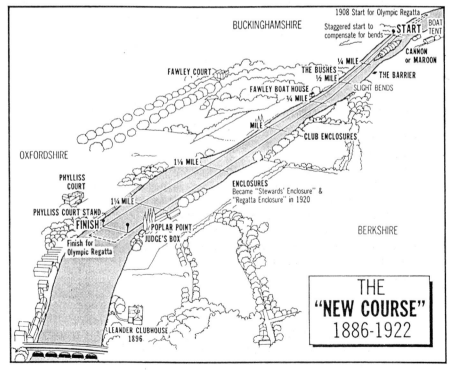

79. The *Henley Royal Regatta* Old and New Course.

It was the Oxford 'blues', the President E. Warre for Eton, and R.W. Risley for Radley, who had most to do with the preliminary negotiations. The Hon. V. Lawless, Captain of Boats at Eton, came to Radley to see Radley's captain, Harry Sewell, and the match was arranged to take place a day or two after Henley Regatta, over the Regatta course.

'The rowing matches at Eton have been suspended since June 14, in consequence of the training necessary for the great struggle with Radley at Henley ...'[28] The race 'created plenty of interest, a certain amount of trouble was taken with the Eight and some discrimination, not too much, was shown in the selection of the crew. Not too much because six out of the seven captains of boats were selected, Denison, captain of the Prince of Wales, or Third Upper, as it was usually called, standing out for medical reasons. The other two were Trench from the Victory and Ricardo from the Britannia, this last choice from a lower boat being regarded as unusual, not to say eccentric'.[29]

From the *Eton Boating Book*:

80. The bays, which were out of the main stream, gave an advantage to the crew on the Berkshire side. They were roped off in 1878 and 1884-85. London Rowing Club, founded 1856, won against Oxford this year, 1857.

... in 1858 a match was made with Radley School to be rowed over the Henley course, and the greatest interest was excited by the reports which were spread about the formidable strength of their Eight. Nobody knew where or what Radley was; but when it was rumoured that they had defeated some College crews at Oxford, and were under the tuition of a well-known oarsman, great anxiety prevailed as to the result of the race. The Eton crew of the year before was one of the heaviest and strongest that had been known in the School, but most of

81. The Henley Regatta in 1858.

the best oars had left, and the Eight selected to row were comparatively light weights. However great faith was reposed in the Captain
of the Boats, who was regarded as one of the most perfect oars ever
seen, and he had won so many of the races, that he was considered
invincible. A very close race was eventually rowed, and the fear of
being beaten by an inferior antagonist was dispelled. [The well-known
oarsman coaching Radley was probably Risley, who was to be in the
Oxford eight a record four years.]

Boating began at Radley soon after its foundation in 1847, but it was
1854 before an eight appeared on the river. So it was a surprising
honour for a school barely a decade old to be challenged by the leading
school in the country, in terms of numbers and prestige, let along
rowing. For this red-letter day in Radley's short history blazers for
the crew were specially designed, incorporating for the first time the
cherry-red 'Maltese' Cross. The jerseys were of flannel, also cerise,
trimmed with white. White straw boaters and white flannel trousers
completed the uniform. (The sight of bare knees was not then considered at all proper. Shorts came in after sliding seats were introduced
in 1872.) A new eight-oar was bought, for which each boy in the school

had to pay ten shillings. The whole school were given leave to go to Henley to support the crew, as happened for the next hundred years and more. Warden Sewell told his audience at the 1872 Old Radleian Dinner: 'I allowed every boy to go whose parents did not object to the expense: I think there were fifty or sixty; but I sent no one but the Prefects to take care of you. Some of the Fellows went to see the Race; but I would have no one but yourselves responsible for your conduct. And yet it was a critical experiment, and a day to me of very great anxiety, for so many contingencies might arise. While you were rowing I was alone in chapel.'

The race was well advertised by notices in the press. 'Considerable interest is created by the great eight-oared race appointed for Saturday evening next over the Henley Regatta course, between the Eton and Radley Schools. The assemblage is expected to be so great that a special train will be run to and fro by the Great Western Railway'.[30]

Boat-Race at Henley between Eton & Radley Schools

Nothing contributes so much to the maintenance of high discipline, combined with gentlemanly feeling, in our public schools as the participation of the masters in the sports and out-door amusements of their pupils. The great and peculiar feature in these establishments is that the boys are educated from their earliest years without that constant supervision, out of school hours, which is thought necessary in private schools; and to effect this most desirable object a high feeling of honour must be instilled, upon which dependence must be placed to prevent those excesses which might otherwise be expected. Now we all know that the fear of punishment alone will not prevent error, which requires also the hope of reward; and it has long been ascertained by experience that nothing is so likely to enlist the youth of this country in the proper path as the permission to embark in manly sports held out as the reward, the punishment being connected with its withdrawal. Boat-racing at Eton has for many years being one of the chief of those introduced into the list of sports there; and until very lately the Westminster School has rivalled the Etonians in this healthful and exciting amusement, an annual race between the two schools having been the culminating point; but from some unexplained causes, the permission has been withdrawn by the master of Westminster, so that Eton has been induced to accept the challenge of the new school at Radley, near Abingdon, which has been established with a special view towards a preparation for Oxford. This bold defiance by so small a body (as compared with Eton, being only 150 to 600) met with a hearty response, and, as a consequence, the race which we are now chronicling was arranged. An attempt was made to bring it off during the late regatta; but the masters very properly came to the conclusion that they should not be able to answer for their charges if the latter were allowed to mix with the general spectators of a regatta. This determination was, in our opinion, most wise and prudent, and it was decided to bring nearly the whole of the Eton boys to Henley. Nothing could be more orderly than the conduct of the disciples of the two schools, who mustered on the banks 500 strong; and we were delighted with the share of interest by the authorities, both before and after the contest. A special train was chartered from Eton and filled with about 450 boys,

82. The Eton VIII 1858 which
beat Radley by 3/4 length in 8
minutes at Henley.
Stereoscopic photographs by
Poulton Photo.

while Radley was contented to take advantage of that which was intended for the general public. Special trains were run from Twyford to meet the fast trains each way, which do not generally stop there, so that the journey was accomplished from London by those who left at four o'clock. At a quarter to six o'clock the first gun was fired, soon after which Radley put in an appearance, the crew rowing down to the island exactly at six o'clock. Their stroke is extremely finished, even in paddling, and shows that great pains have been taken in coaching them. Their average age being somewhat below that of the Eton crew, two being only fourteen years old, it is not to be wondered at that they row with less power, but their time is excellent, and the uniformity of style is highly to be commended; indeed, but for this they would stand no chance with their competitors. We understand that Mr Austin, who rowed the stroke oar, has only lately undertaken that difficult office, an impediment existing to the carrying out of the original selection in consequence of a medical opinion forbidding it from prudential motives. The No. 3 also was suffering from enlarged glands, owing to an inflamed tooth, and we most of us know how these disagreeables interfere with the high state of health required for such a struggle as was here maintained. On the appearance of the Etonians it was at once evident to the practised eye that Radley was overmatched in strength, and that on an even course, with equally good rowing and pluck, the red and white must succumb to light blue; but the former, having the Berks shore, might hope to be able to keep their water to themselves and thus eventually pull through, in imitation of the Cambridge with the Londoners. The Hon. Mr Lawless rows a splendid oar, and his crew back him up exactly after the same model, though not all perhaps quite attaining his degree of excellence. Neither of these crews have the strength to take as deep a hold of the water as their older compeers at the Universities; but the Etonians in particular are very 'quick

83. The Radley VIII 1858 at
Bird Place where, in the early
years of the Regatta, crews
kept their boats and embarked
from the lawn.

through,' even allowing for the fact that they do not quite cover their
blades. Moreover, there is not the slightest shirking amongst them,
and every back is as straight as an arrow, with the thumb well against
the ribs in bringing the oar home. We may, therefore, congratulate the
two schools on possessing as fine a crew each as they are likely to see
for some years. The boats were both built for the occasion – that of Eton
by Matthew Taylor, and the Radley craft by King, of Oxford, but as
nearly as may be after Taylor's model. The latter is very small, as of
course is required by such a light crew, and indeed, we fancied her
scarcely floaty enough; but we understand King's orders were impera-
tive to build her as small and as light as possible, and here he has
succeeded, as she is barely a hundred weight and a half, and is only 54
feet long. The Etonians rowed in white Jerseys edged with light blue,
the Radleys in red edged with white, so that there was no difficulty in
distinguishing the two at any distance, from the contrast between the
colours.

A steady breeze off the Bucks shore was supposed to be slightly in
favour of the boat having that station, but as the river is nearly
bank-full, and the wind was not strong enough to make the water at
all lumpy, we do not imagine that the difference was appreciable. Mr
Chitty, of the University of Oxford, well-known as the stroke of
"Chitty's four", was chosen as umpire, which duty he performed on
horseback, but as there was not the slightest approach to a foul, his
office was fortunately a sinecure. We have no doubt, however, that if
such an event had taken place, he would have been even more able to
detect its nature from the saddle than from the stern of an eight oar.
    At a quarter past six both boats were at their respective stations,
and in a short time a good start was effected, Eton at once getting into
full swing in the most splendid style, and soon drawing away, so that

at the end of a quarter of a mile she was three-quarters of a length ahead. Here Radley put on the steam, and by hard rowing she lessened the gap; but the Etonians again put their backs to their work, and opposite Remenham had regained the original distance and something more, their stern nearly clearing the bows of their opponent's boat. From this point to the Poplars the struggle was most desperate, and the shouts on the bank proportionately loud, Radley being badly represented in point of numbers, and therefore less vociferously cheered than Eton. On reaching the point, the coxswain of the Etonians, finding it impracticable to take the Berkshire water, did not make the attempt, and kept a course nearly mid stream, Radley rounding the point in good style, and thereby gaining some distance, but nevertheless still unable quite to reach her stronger opponent. On entering the straight water below the barges, Radley was about a third of her length behind Eton, and the two went in with most determined rowing on both sides; but it was here evident that the Etonians were the stronger, as was proved by their improving their position as soon as they were on even terms, winning finally by half a boat's length, or possibly a trifle more. Nothing could be more plucky than the rowing of the Radley crew; and, considering the changes so recently made in them and their greater youth, we think their coming so near to Eton is a great feather in their cap. The time, as taken by us, was 7 min. 55 seconds. After the crews left their boats, the captain of the winning boat was chaired through the town to his quarters, on reaching which the losing crew were also warmly received, the Etonians leading the cheering. Soon afterwards both schools were conveyed to their destinations by their respective trains, apparently highly delighted with the prowess of their champion crews. *The Field* (3 July 1858)

The two fourteen year olds in the Radley crew were Monsell at bow and Phillips at 6 '... an impediment existing to the carrying out of the original selection in consequence of a medical opinion forbidding it from prudential motives' means that Harry Sewell (nephew of the Warden) was forbidden to row by the doctor. This would have been a severe loss. He had been in the Eight for four years. 'In the old days stroke and captain were synonyms ... The stroke was elected by the club. He was supposed to be the best all-round oar, and as such to be capable of setting the best stroke to the crew. His office attached itself to his seat ... At Eton the traditional law of identity of stroke and captain held good until 1864'.[31]

As the crews never had daylight between them, Eton was unable to take Radley's water and so counter the advantage of the Berkshire station at the bend. In those days, and until 1872, a crew which took their opponents' water was entitled to keep it; in fact it had to keep it. The overtaken crew had to move over towards the opposite bank when it tried to overtake in its turn.

Sir,
Your admirably-penned report of the spirited contest between the scholars of Eton and Radley cannot fail to be read with deep interest, and I trust the representatives of the two schools may henceforth meet annually in generous rivalry on the Thames, and evince the same skill and manliness which marked the struggle of both crews in the late

contest. I doubt not Eton will ever strive to maintain her ancient prestige; and may the sons of that youthful institution, St Peter's College, Radley, which promises to be an ornament to this country, relax no efforts in securing for their Alma Mater that renown which their energetic Warden, Dr Sewell, is anxious to promote, in everything that relates to sound scholarship, sterling manliness of character, and gentlemanly bearing. I simply wish to correct an error in your report, and to explain that in the late challenge the gauntlet was thrown down by the Etonians.
Olim Etonensis

Bell's Life in London reported 'an immense concourse of fashionables amounting to at least 4000 persons: indeed the bridge and the meadows presented much the same appearance as on regatta day.' If the boys and the 'fashionables' did amount to 4000 persons, they just about equalled the then population of Henley. Other press estimates were lower.

The most significant name in the Radley Eight is W. B. ('Guts') Woodgate, who was to develop into the greatest oarsman of his day. After his 'blue' at Oxford (where he founded Vincent's Club) he won the Wingfield Sculls (Amateur Championship) at Putney three times, and the Grand, the Stewards', the Silver Goblets, the Visitors', and the Diamond Sculls at Henley. In 1862 he rowed five times on one day, winning three events but losing in the final of the Diamonds in a re-row after a dead-heat. A noted eccentric, he invented Coxless Fours at Henley by telling his cox, who could not swim, to jump into the river at the start of the race. (They won, but were disqualified.)

In his *Reminiscences of an Old Sportsman* he wrote: 'It was not until my last summer (1858) that I first managed to gain a seat in the first eight, and to row in a match v. Eton at Henley on the Saturday after Henley regatta. I was No. 2, 9st 5lb – and the worst oar in the boat. John Xavier Merriman, now Cape Premier, was our Henley No. 5. Merriman was a good six feet high when he came to Radley, barely fifteen … I myself was undeniably stunted in growth by my limited sleep hours. When I reached Oxford I scaled well under 10 st.! I began to grow then, and in due time reached about 12 st. fighting weight.' In subsequent encounters with Eton at Henley up to the First World War, Eton's weight and strength always prevailed, but in 1858 the Radley crew was just the heavier by 2 lb a man. The striking difference in weight between then and now is illustrated by the Exeter Eight which was Head of the River at Oxford. They averaged 10 st 2lb, exactly the same as Radley.

Woodgate in the *Badminton Library Boating* (1888) includes the new boat, in which he himself rowed, among the historical keelless eight-oars and gives the details as 'Length 56ft 0in., Beam 2ft 0 3/4in, Depth at stern 7 1/2in.' Two years earlier, in 1856 Matt Taylor of Newcastle built the first smooth keelless, cedar hull for eights, which Clasper had before invented for smaller craft on the Tyne. In this boat Royal Chester Boat Club caused a sensation at Henley by winning both the Grand and the Ladies' Plate. From then on clinker-built (overlapping) hulls gave way to keeless carvel (flush) ones. It was Taylor who built the Eton boat.

> The rowing of both crews was much admired, the style of the Etonians being perhaps the liveliest of the two; the colours of Eton were pale or Cambridge blue, and of Radley, red and white, and the two crews, in their new boats and elegant uniforms, certainly looked 'A 1.' ... The rowing on both sides was very capital and severe. *Jackson's Oxford Journal*

Eton's colours of Cambridge blue should more properly be Cambridge's colours of Eton blue. At the second University Boat Race in 1836 Oxford appeared with dark blue colours, and Cambridge, having none of their own, adopted the light blue of their Etonian oarsmen, a piece of Eton Blue ribbon bought from a nearby shop just before the start being fixed to the bows.

> The rowing was scientific and vigorous in both boats, and the shouts of the assembled multitude might have been heard for miles. The exertions of these gentlemen will be duly appreciated when we state that the time occupied in the race was only eight minutes, while the picked crew of the Cambridge University, who defeated the great London Rowing Club on Tuesday week, with more favourable wind, occupied seven minutes and a half. Mr Chitty (than whom a finer oarsman never existed) ... as there was no crew to be found at Henley who could keep pace with the combatants ... performed the duty on horseback, perhaps not the most felicitous mode if anything very particular had occurred. *The Morning Post*

Umpires at the Regatta were rowed by a crew of Thames Watermen, the Umpire holding the rudder-lines. Four years before: 'On the next day the appearance of the river was greatly enlivened by the Eton eight in their uniform of light blue, and in one of the heats they good-naturedly carried the Umpire' (*Bell's Life* in 1854). (It was customary to wear blazers, long ones in Eton's case, in the boat when not racing.) In 1868 the crews of watermen who carried the umpires were unable to keep up in many of the races. Next year a steam-launch was first used in their place.

> A very large party of aquatic gentlemen, members of the great clubs, visited Henley to view the contest ... Vast number of persons crowded the starting post, the assemblage being little less than on the second day of the regatta, and the excitement depicted on the countenances of many was indescribable ... the Eton gentlemen came in first, with the nose of the Radley boat exactly level with the coxswain of the Eton's. *The Berkshire Chronicle*

If the race was conducted according to the rules then in force at the Regatta, it was not the 'nose' (bow) of the boat which was important, but the tail (stern).

In 1857, in consequence of the Chester ship being some dozen feet shorter than the iron keeled craft of Exeter and Lady Margaret, a question arose as to how the boats should be adjudicated past the post. The boats started by *sterns*, therefore Chester would be giving several feet start if adjudged at the finish by bows. So the stewards ordered the races to be decided by *sterns* past the post. This edict remained in force, but unknown to the majority of competitors, till after 1864. In that year the winner of the Diamonds reached the post several lengths before his opponent, but stopped opposite to it in a stiff head wind. The loser came up behind him leisurely, chatted, and shoved the winner past the post by rowlocks locking. Presently it transpired that the official fiat was 'won by a foot,' and that the judge did not consider the race over until the winner's stern was clear of the line! This discovery caused some inquiry, and the half-forgotten edict of 1857 was thus repealed; and races have since then been adjudged again by bows. W.B.Woodgate, *Boating*

A Radley eye-witness at Henley was the Sub-Warden (later Warden) William Wood, who reported in his diary

... In the afternoon went down to Henley to see the Race. The course is very pretty. Few Radleians. Eton came down in great force, 550 boys by special train! All in beaver and blue ties and blue ribbons! A second Thermopylae it looked like, tried in vain to feel composed but the suspense was great and painful till the actual start. A glorious race. They got off better than Radley but we gradually pulled up to them and kept our place, coming in with our bows at their stroke oar. Tremendous enthusiasm. The Etonians carried their captain over the bridge to the Hotel. They behaved well and cheered Radley. Had a lunch for Radley and Austin [Chief Coach. Elder brother of stroke. Oxford crew 1858]. proposed the eight.

Beavers were tall hats of real or imitation beaver fur. The Radleians wore straw boaters. Wood later recalled: 'Meeting a well-known Oxford tradesman after the race, who was somewhat of a sporting character, I said: "Didn't the Radley fellows row well?" "Ah!" replied the hatter, "but wasn't it a grand sight to see those Eton gentlemen filing over the Bridge, many 'underds of them, and every one in a top 'at?"'

An Etonian account of the race appeared twelve years later in *Recollections of Eton* by C.F. Johnstone (1870).

'By this day next week,' I said, 'we shall have won our race.'
'What do you mean?' he asked.
'Why, our race with Radley, of course.'
'Oh, yes, at Henley. It's almost a dead certainty; we must win. But all the same, you know,' he added, 'I think it was foolish of us ever to accept their challenge. We might perfectly have declined it, and told them they were too insignificant. But now we have begun it, it will have to go on every year.'
'Yes, I see what you mean; we've nothing to gain and everything to lose.'

'That's just it.It does us no credit beating them, and if by any chance they won, we should be frightfully disgraced.'
'Oh, but they won't win.'
'I don't think they can,' replied Mason, 'but we shall see.'

There was a good deal of excitement in the school generally about this race. Since the contest with Westminster had been done away with, our eight had no annual struggle whatever to stimulate them to exertion. Radley, however, had challenged us this year, and though many of the Eton multitude had never heard of the place before, it was determined to accept the defiance. The next question was where it was to be rowed, and after some consultation Henley was agreed upon, and the time fixed to be the day after the regatta, which would take place there in the middle of June.

How the school was to see it was another thing which perplexed the authorities. But considering that it would not be on one of the actual days of the regatta itself, it was at last settled with unparalleled magnanimity that every one should be allowed to go, and that a special train should convey the boys from Eton thither.

This was made known to us formally, together with the time at which we were to start, on the day before the race. We were all of us to be ready the next day after three o'clock school, and meet at the Great Western Station. There was no fear that any of us would fail to be there, and accordingly the moment school was over we rushed up to secure our places in the train.

The station which we got out at was close to the river, and it took us a very short time to get into the main street, and then over the bridge and down on to the river bank. The two crews had not come on the water yet, for it was barely half-past five, and the race was not to be rowed before six, so we all of us loitered about on the bank, and surveyed the course until they came.

'Oh, yes, there's no doubt that the Henley scenery is nearly the best on the Thames; but looking at it simply as a course for a race, it is rather spoilt by that sharp turn above the Poplars.'
'Well, I suppose it is; it gives the inside boat an immense advantage.'

Before the boats appeared, our ranks received an unexpected addition of spectators. The Radley boys came down like ourselves to see the race. There were of course not nearly so many of them as there were Etonians, and indeed they might have been altogether overlooked in the crowd, had not the red rosette which they all wore proclaimed them to be none of us. We turned to look upon them as they came by, and they turned to look at us; and no doubt in the spirit of schoolboy rivalry neither of us thought very much of the other. But our attention was soon taken up by the two eights as they came out from their place of shelter, and rowed past the admiring crowds. Eton of course received the most cheering, because there were so many more lungs to contribute to it; and to myself as well as to all the rest of us, they certainly appeared to be the neatest crew.

Nearly everybody went down with them to the start, intending to run along the bank with the race. But Lovell and I only walked on a little way in the direction by which they were to come.

'Those fellows who run all the way,' he observed, 'won't see the finish. But look here, I believe they're off.'

'Yes, I hear the shouting; but I can't make them out yet.'

'There they are,' he said, after a few moments' pause. 'There, you can see them; and what's more, I see the light blue oars on the outside.'

'Then they've got this Berkshire side, and get the advantage of the turn. What a bore!'

'Never mind,' he said, 'we shall be all right; we'll take their water before that.'

'I'll tell you what, we must keep up here so as to see them. Eton are ahead now, I can make that out.'

'I don't know that,' he said, 'they look almost level.'

'Here they come now,' I cried. 'Now we shall see them.' As they came on towards us, we could see that Eton was putting on a violent spurt, in hopes probably of being able to take the Radley water, as we had prophesied, and so get the advantage at the fatal corner.

'Now we must run on,' said Lovell. 'Come on before the crowd.'

Boats, runners, and ourselves all left the Poplars behind, and tore on, eager to see how the spurt would carry the blue oars forward. Shouts of "Well rowed, Eton!" mixed with fainter ones of "Now then, Radley!" attested the interest which was taken in the contest. The uproar became louder and louder as each boat seemed to increase or lessen its distance. Eton rowed most manfully; but the attempt to take the Berkshire side was rather too much for it, and Radley kept her advantage,and came round the corner and up to us hand over hand.

There was no longer a certainty of our winning, the chances seemed growing less and less, and the despairing shouts and exhortations from the bank told that some of us foresaw the possibility of our disgrace. Radley drew on, with every appearance of passing us, but the spirits of our own crew were so stirred at the prospect, that they strained every nerve to keep their position. The red oars came up, but never quite got level; the appearance of success was fortunately but temporary, still the danger was by no means over. Both at last put on the final spurt; the powers of Eton then told, and as they came past the post the blue oars were the winners by three-quarters of a length.

'That was unpleasantly near,' said Mason, as soon as the cheers and shouting had subsided.

'Yes, that it was,' I answered. 'I'm sure they can't have such an eight every year.'

'No, I heard that it was because it was a better one than usual that they had sent the challenge.'

'Well, now we must go and give them an ovation as they come on to the bridge.'

A crowd had assembled, but it was some time before the heroes of the day made their appearance. When at length they did present themselves, the storm of cheers that greeted them was such as Henley had never before in all probability heard. A hoisting took place at once, as if we had been in the midst of Eton, and the whole crowd moved in a body up the town.

'Where are they going to?' asked Parker.

'Aune, nune incumbile nemus.'

84. Eton v. Radley at Henley 1858.

Why, to the inn, you know. It's the Catherine Wheel, some way up the street.'

The sort of hero worship which boys always show prompted the whole school to follow their eight as far as the inn, and then to congregate outside it in a sort of way that showed the highest veneration for those who were within. The Captain of the Boats was looked upon as a perfect sovereign by his assembled subjects, especially after the triumph he had gained; and all waited for his appearance at the window with an eagerness that would hardly have been shown for royalty. At last he appeared, and made a sort of speech from the balcony, which reminded one forcibly of a Windsor election. Not that the topics were the same, for it was a sort of short eulogy on boating in general and these two crews in particular, but the hotel window and the crowd outside looked uncommonly parliamentary. After this was over, and the cheers for both eights had subsided, our crowd dispersed; most of us to seek some refreshment in the inns until the time came for our return to Windsor.

The next year, 1859, Radley challenged Eton in their turn, but were refused, being told that 'Eton did not intend to row any more such matches with Radley.' In *Memories of Eton & Etonians* (1899), Alfred Lubbock writes of the Eton Eight of 1858: '... it only averaged ten stone ... but was a fairly good crew. The Eight of 1859 was an exceptionally bad one ... very light, and had but little coaching ... I think that three or four ... including C.A. Wynne, the Captain, would hardly have been considered good enough for any Eton eight of the present day.' Wynne was the only survivor from 1858. *Wood's Diary* of 28th March 1859 reveals that there was correspondence between the headmasters. 'In evening College Meeting ... The Warden read us Goodford's letter and his own. We agreed with him that as Eton is reluctant we could not possibly press our right to a return match, but wished his own letter had given fewer reasons and kept nearer to the right one.'

Henley Royal Regatta

Despite the rejection of the challenge, it was not long before Eton and Radley were again opposed at Henley. In 1857, following the success of Royal Chester in the previous year, the Rules of Entry for the Ladies' Challenge Plate[32] had limited entrants to Oxford and Cambridge college clubs and the schools of Eton and Westminster. In 1861 Eton entered, and Radley too were accepted. Doubtless Radley's fine performance in 1858 encouraged the Stewards' Committee to waive the Rules. Westminster did not enter because the timing of their Whitsun holiday did not allow them sufficient days to prepare. They first entered for the Ladies' Plate in 1922.

'When first approached on the subject of Henley Regatta, Dr Goodford [Headmaster of Eton 1853-62] had expressed an opinion that it would be useless for mere boys to contend against trained crews of University men.'[33] The race with Radley over the Henley Regatta course with the flattering press comments may have persuaded Dr Goodford. But in all probability it was the return to Eton, as a master, in 1860, of Edmond Warre that was the deciding factor. Woodgate in Boating wrote: 'It was with his assistance that Dr Goodford was persuaded to allow the eight to go to Henley Regatta in 1861.' Alfred Lubbock was at Eton from 1854-63: 'I believe it was chiefly through Mr Warre that the race with Westminster was revived this year.' (1860). One wonders how much the race with Radley was a means to both these ends. In arranging this match Warre's friendship with Robert Risley must have been a factor. (Warre and Risley were two of the six undergraduates, who with six dons were the mainstay of the Oxford University Rifle Volunteer Corps, which was founded at Warre's lodgings in 1859 at a time of national fear of a French invasion.) Risley was in the 1858 Eight of which Warre was President. It was Warre who had the idea of staging Oxford Trial Eights for the first time in 1858, from the bend above Abingdon Lasher to Nuneham island. No doubt here he came across Radley oarsmen, and possibly Dr Sewell. It is reasonable to surmise that the Old Etonian 'Olim Etonensis', who corrected *The Field* with his flattering remarks about Radley and Sewell, was Edmond Warre.

The Eton Boating Book shows Warre's influence on Eton rowing. '... two epochs in our rowing, the first up to 1840, when it was disreputable and unrecognised, the second the score of years during which it was acquiesced in and then recognised to the extent that in 1847 the Headmaster did not disdain to witness a race. A third began when the masters themselves took an active part. But this change came slowly. For a score of years after his return as a master in 1860

Dr Warre was practically alone on the towpath.' Alfred Lubbock wrote: 'On the coming of Mr Warre to Eton as an assistant master ... the whole tone and form of the rowing underwent a vast change and improvement, chiefly through his instrumentality. He also gave a lot of his spare time to coaching and rowing with the Eight.' Warre was not however the official coach. He was an adviser to the Captain of Boats, and only coached when asked to do so. Surprisingly, Warre himself was never a member of the Eton Eight. Perhaps this influenced his thinking. For the match with Westminster at Putney in 1860, 'The steps which the new coach took were startling: he threw seniority to the winds; the Captain of the Lower Boats was discarded with other senior choices, and others were selected who were never thought of as having a shadow of a chance. The result fully justified his judgment.'[34] Warre's benign influence on Eton rowing was to have the opposite effect on Radley Eights at Henley from 1861 onwards, as well as ending the Westminster challenge lower down the river. In 1884 Dr Warre was appointed Headmaster of Eton, which office he held until 1905.

Eton and Radley remained the only schools to compete for the Ladies' Plate until 1877, when Cheltenham made their first appearance. In the early years it was a very uneven contest. Eton were a match, and more than a match for the Oxford and Cambridge colleges, winning the Ladies' Plate five times in the 1860s and seven times in the '90s. In contrast Radley struggled. 'Plucky', 'pretty', and 'gamely', are words used by the press to describe their unavailing efforts to defeat heavier and more experienced opponents.

In their first year at the Regatta, 1861, they rowed against First Trinity, Cambridge, the eventual winners, and Eton. With no booms down the course there was room for three crews rowing abreast. At the start, when the unfortunate Radley cox, Cecil Hook, dropped the bung line, it fouled the rudder and lost the crew several strokes. As a result of this accident stakeboats were introduced the next year, with men to hold the boats' sterns replacing the bung lines. Among the witnesses of Radley's misfortune was William Oliver, who had been in the Lower School at Eton, which he found less restrictive than Radley.

> In the years 1861, 1862, the Radley eight rowed for the 'Ladies' Plate' at Henley Regatta in June. The whole school used to go over there in three four-horse drags, and fine fun we had of it; the thirty miles' drive over such pretty country as the Oxford and Henley road seemed to do one an immense deal of good after the way we were penned in at that old convent.
>
> In 1862, coming back [near Benson] one of the drags had a spill, the fore-wheel coming off; luckily this happened at the very spot where it did, or life would have been lost; had it happened fifty yards sooner or later, they would have had a roll down an embankment with probably the drag on top of them. As it was there were some severe bruises and sprains, but no one seemed to care much, as of course the prospect of being regarded as heroes for the next eight days or so covered it all.[35]

From the following year the railway was used instead.

In 1865 some lines in a poem in the *Radleian* drew the scorn of the *Eton College Chronicle*:

> Oh may that glorious day soon come
> When the plucky Radley crew
> Their colours red and white, shall leave
> Behind the faded blue.
>
> ————
>
> Then why don't these brave oarsmen
> Send Henley such a crew
> As shall show real proof of power
> And leave 'the faded blue',
> Instead of vainly boasting
> They will win the Ladies' Plate
> And distance the Etonians
> With Radley's *little weight*.

Radley won the tiniest of victories in 1867 when Eton reached the final of the Grand and scratched to concentrate on the Ladies' Plate, where Radley were their opponents. *The Eton Boating Book* recorded magnanimously: 'Radley have never beaten Eton, but they may say that on this occasion Eton was afraid of them.' *The Athletic Review* echoed this view: 'Great things had been expected of the Radleians ... Radley had a momentary advantage and held the lead till the bottom of the bay ... Eton all the way rowing at the tremendous pace of from 45 to 50 strokes per minute' won by 3 lengths in the same time as the Grand. Eton have never won the Grand, but have reached the final three times, including the last time they entered in 1908.

In 1868 Radley beat a crew for the first time at Henley, when they switched to the Thames Cup and came second to Pembroke, Oxford, but ahead of London R.C. 2nd VIII. In 1870 they won their first heat, against the Royal Artillery, but again only in the Thames Cup. The school was going through a bad patch, and numbers fell below 80 in the 1870s. *The Field* in 1871: 'It seems almost a pity that Radley should send a crew to Henley year after year without any prospect of success. Indeed we question whether it would not be sounder policy not to send a crew at all, unless it was an exceptionally good one.' *The Radleian* endorsed this view: 'There is nothing particularly "plucky" in sending up a bad eight; indeed it seems little else than foolhardy, considering what the expense is and what little return there is for it.'

In three years no crew was entered for the Regatta. In 1877 Cheltenham entered for the Ladies' Plate, asking to be drawn against Radley. The Stewards refused the request, but they allowed a private match at the Regatta. Radley won 'by about 4 lengths of daylight' and were rewarded with medals presented by the Regatta. '... the Cheltenham boys appearing very fagged ... It transpired afterwards that the losers had come over from Reading after an early breakfast and had eaten nothing since. Boys are not like men, and want food when in an excited state, like on a regatta day' (*Land & Water*).

Cheltenham had their revenge two years later when they defeated Radley in a new event, the Public Schools Challenge Cup for Fours. Bedford won this in 1880 and 1881, in the latter year beating Radley and Westminster in the Final, in what became known as the Mutton Fat Race. The *Westminster Town Boy Ledger* wrote: 'Radley had a very good crew and rowed well together. It would have been some consolation if they had won instead of Bedford who went and evaded the rule of fixed seats by having their seats greased with mutton fat and sliding on it.' 'Sliding seats being forbidden in this race, the Bedford crew at the instigation of their boat builder, had wide seats, which they greased and slid upon.'[36]

In fact, Bedford had cleared their action with the Regatta Secretary before the race; but the Henley Stewards decided that, while this conformed to the letter of the law, it did not conform to its spirit, and from the next year they limited the width of a thwart to six inches. Magdalen College School, Hereford School, Derby School and Bedford Modern were subsequent winners before the Public Schools Cup migrated to Marlow Regatta in 1886. Cheltenham disappeared from Henley in 1881, not returning until 1951. Bedford first competed there in Eights in 1886. In 1882 Radley beat First Trinity, Cambridge in a heat of the Ladies', and as there were only four entries they were in the final against Eton, who won by 3 lengths. In 1884 a fancied Christ Church crew was beaten by 2 lengths, but once again in the final Eton were too strong.

In 1891 'a tremendous race' was rowed with Eton who won by half a length. In 1893 Radley won a heat against Bedford School and then 'boylicked' Trinity, Oxford, and were again in the final against Eton – who won by 3 lengths. Press reports were complimentary: 'The Ladies' Plate showed us the best rowing of the whole Regatta in our opinion and that was in the final heat between the Public Schools of Eton and Radley.' 'With regard to the boys it is not too much to say that they were the two best crews at the Regatta. They might not be able to beat the Leander or some others, because age, weight, and experience would tell, but there were none which rowed in so good a style, or which were so thoroughly well together.'

Chapter 7

Late Nineteenth-Century Games

Fives, cricket and football were the games played most widely at public schools in the first half of the 19th century. Other games were introduced in the latter part of the century. Hockey is a later English version of the stick games played in Ireland and Scotland. The name is not found until the late 18th century. About Byron, who was at Harrow from 1801 to 1805, one of his school-fellows said 'Though Byron was lame he was a great lover of sports, and preferred hockey to Horace, relinquished even Helicon for Duck-puddle and gave up the best poet that ever wrote hard Latin for a game of cricket on the

85. *Fives at Leicester Fields*. Despite the title, a game of Rackets played in a tennis Court, 1788.

common.'[1] Hockey is now mostly played at schools in the early months of the year. This was the period between the end of the football season and the beginning of the cricket season that schools had most difficulty in filling when the school year was divided into two 'halves'.

Athletic sports was one brief solution to the problem. This was one of several individual, as opposed to team, sports that gained popularity in the later decades of the century. The first school Gymnasium was built at Uppingham in 1859, closely followed by Radley's in 1860. Gymnastics, as well as Boxing and Fencing, were encouraged by the Public Schools Gymnastics, Boxing and Fencing Competitions held annually at Aldershot, the formation of Officer Training Corps at many schools being the rationale. For the same reason Rifle Shooting became a competitive school sport. From 1862 the Ashburton Shield was shot for at Wimbledon, initially by Eton, Harrow, Winchester, Marlborough, Cheltenham, Rugby and Rossall. But the individual game that was and remains pre-eminently a public school game – to however limited an extent – is Rackets.

Rackets

Rackets in its strictly modern form is a comparatively new game ... It is impossible to find a single reference to Rackets before 1800.[2]

First came fives played with the hand. Then came Bat Fives. That was a good game; and it is still played in many places and notably at some of our great schools ... Not content with the wooden bat, players acquainted with the tennis-racket seem to have adapted that instrument about 1749, or a little earlier ... and it was still then called Fives. In the 18th century it was popular in the prisons of the Fleet and King's Bench, and later in the gardens of some of the great London taverns, such as the Belvidere in Pentonville, the Eagle, White Conduit House, and the Bear at Kennington. In all these places the game was played in the open – that is, unroofed – courts, which doubtless replaced or imitated former fives courts ... The first name of a regular champion of which any record exists is that of Robert Mackay 1820 ...

At Harrow it was certainly not played before 1822 or 1823, when the new wing was added to the old building. When the new wing was completed, the yard was levelled, and covered with gravel; this was then kept rolled and smooth, and any misguided boys who were caught running across it, wearing heeled shoes, were fined a shilling each. These fines helped to pay for rolling the ground. The balls were large, called 'best fives', and covered with buff leather; the rackets then used were old tennis-rackets cut down and made lighter ... This information is contributed by one who was an eye-witness in 1826. At that time, the Balls and rackets were sold by an old woman named Arnold, commonly known as 'Old Polly'.

The first court at Harrow was merely a gravelled floor, at the foot of a high wall, which was perforated with many windows. These were protected by wire-netting, and the rebound of the ball was frequently deflected in most unexpected directions by the carved mouldings and other ornamental excrescences, with which the surface of the wall was

86. The Fleet Prison ... was originally so called from the river Fleet running by it ...
The inner court, where the prisoners entertain themselves with tennis,fives
[rackets, in fact], and other amusements, as represented in the plate ... The rooms
measure fourteen feet and a half by twelve and a half ... The number of prisoners
usually confined in the Fleet is about two hundred and fifty, and the number who
have the benefit of the rules is about fifty more ... This prison belongs to the Court
of Common Pleas and hither persons are committed for contempt of orders &c. in
the High Court of Chancery; or upon debt when by a writ of habeas corpus they
remove themselves thither from any other prison ... The rules or liberties of the
Fleet are, all the north side of Ludgate-hill, and the Old Bailey up to Fleet-lane;
down that lane into the market, and then turning the corner on the left all the east
side along the Fleet Prison to the bottom of Ludgate-hill. W.H. Pyne. Rowlandson &
Pugin del^t. et sculp^t. (1808), *Microcosm of London*

varied. Yet this was the best court at Harrow for many years, and
immensely prized by the boys. It was sacred to the sixth form, and to
those who might be invited to play there as a special favour. New
courts were built in 1851, on the slope below the school-yard and
'milling ground', but still without roofs, though walled in. They were
too broad and not very satisfactory in other respects. About twelve or

87. The King's Bench Prison ... is a place of confinement for debtors, and for those sentenced by the court of King's Bench for libels and other misdemeanors; but such as are able to purchase the liberties, may have the benefit of walking through a part of the Borough and in St George's fields. The walls of the prison are very high, and all prospect beyond them is excluded even from the uppermost windows ... The rooms measure about 9 feet square ... Prisoners from any other gaol may be removed to this by habeas corpus. W.H. Pyne. Rowlandson & Pugin del[t.] et sculp[t.] (1808), *Microcosm of London*

thirteen years later the present covered court was built. J. Spens & J. Marshall & J.A. Tait (1890), *Tennis, Rackets, Fives*

The Rev. H.J. Torre, who was at Harrow from 1831, recalls:

Except rackets there was no other games than cricket and football at Harrow in those days ... Almost every boarding-house at Harrow had its miniature racket Court, in which a game with a soft india-rubber ball is played. It so chances that nearly all the houses have a part where a blank wall runs at right angles to another ... A sheet of asphalte is then laid. H.J. Torre (1890), *Recollections of School Days at Harrow*

PIERCE EGAN'S
BOOK OF SPORTS.

No. XV.]   [*Price Three Pence.*

THE GAME OF RACKETS:
One of the most healthful Exercises connected with BRITISH SPORTS;
and the principal Amusement for confined debtors in the
FLEET *and* KING'S BENCH *Prisons:*

88. 'At rackets, the ball is struck against what is called a head-wall, and returned at the bound to the same wall. During the Swellish times, as they have been since termed by those persons who were in the habit of "making money" by the rich debtors ... the Game of Rackets was in high estimation, and very large sums of money were lost and won upon it. The King's Bench Prison at that period [the turn of the century] was one continued scene of *gaiety* and *dash* – indeed, it was like any thing else but a place of confinement. The promenade, almost every evening, until the cry of "all out" occurred, was a complete picture of *le beau monde*. It exhibited some of the most elegant dressed females in the kingdom; the finest, nay, fashionable women who felt not the slightest reproach by visiting their unfortunate friends in "durance vile" ... The game of rackets was carried on with great spirit ... and the ground was frequently covered with visitors of the most elegant description to witness the trials of skill. The game of rackets in the Fleet and King's Bench Prisons has often turned out a source of livelihood to a number of the prisoners who have been attached to the sport ... A man of the name of Hoskins, who was at one period of his confinement [in the King's Bench Prison] the *racket-master*, a capital player, and who altered the game from 11 to 15, ... waiting upon gentlemen [prisoners and visitors] with the bats and balls, and frequently taking a hand in a match, he was enabled to support his family of seven children ... He was a Cornish man, and of very good family; his father was a respectable surgeon, and Hoskins was brought up a gentleman; he was here at the suit of a single creditor, one whom he once called friend and benefactor, and for a disputed debt which he vowed he would never pay. He was a good tempered, convivial, amiable, and benevolent man ... he died in December 1823, after an *uninterrupted imprisonment* of Thirty-Eight *years*!!!'

89. The Racket Court at the Belvidere Tavern, Pentonville 1858. 'There are several open Rackets Courts, independent of the King's Bench and the Fleet Prisons … There is a good open Court at the Belvidere, Pentonville; another at the Eagle Tavern in the City Road; and the proprietor of White Conduit House a third; but the fault of these places is that the company is not sufficiently select, and that a gentleman who is fond of the game (and all are fond of it who can play at all) are there compelled to join a miscellany of very respectable persons no doubt, but not of the highest grade in society. As it is, the ardour of some individuals of rank and education in pursuit of the game induces them to overlook the inconvenience to which we have alluded, and we must do the proprietors of the Courts we have named the justice to say, that they contrive to keep persons of really, questionable character and appearance at a distance'. *Pierce Egan's Book of Sports* (1832)

The detailed description of the ball in each account seems to show that Harrow was not only the nursery for the game of Rackets, but also the home of Squash Rackets, a game whose world-wide popularity in the 20th century far exceeds its big brother, played with a hard ball in large, expensive to build courts.

Closed Rackets courts began to be built about 1840. The court at Lord's was built in 1839-40.

90. The rubber ball game at Harrow was known as 'Squash'.

The real turning point in support of the covered court was the opening of Old Princes Club [by two brothers of that name] in 1853. The centre court at Old Princes Club determined the size of all future courts, 60 feet x 30 feet. From the date of institution of Old Princes Club the game gradually ceased to be played in Taverns, the old courts were allowed to fall into decay, and Rackets became the sport of an educated and more wealthy minority. This was both its salvation and its despair. To

91. Old Princes Club (1853-1886), the first enclosed court with four walls. It set the standard for all Rackets Courts and put an end to the Belvidere and similar outdoor courts.

92. The Racquet Court Rugby School with Fives / Squash Courts attached c. 1880. As at other schools, Fives now bows to squash rackets as the most popular small court game.

play well is to jeopardise the life of one's racket ... The number of balls used in a closely contested seven-game match is roughly one hundred. [This was in 1933 but is no longer valid.][3]

Old Princes Club was pulled down in 1886. Queen's Club was opened 1887. In *Tennis, Rackets, Fives* in 1890 the authors had said 'It is rather strange that the laws of rackets have never yet been authoritatively laid down.' In 1894 a written code of Rules appeared. The Tennis & Rackets Association was formed at Queen's Club in 1907.

The game today is dominated by the limited number of Public Schools who possess a court, and by their Old Boys. The Public Schools Championship began in 1868 when Harrow, Eton, Charterhouse and Cheltenham competed; Rugby entered in 1869; Winchester, Haileybury, Wellington and Marlborough in the 1870s; Malvern, Clifton and Radley in the 1880s; Tonbridge, Rossall and Westminster subsequently, although the last two dropped out. At Rossall there was no professional and the court was unsatisfactory. It was later converted into squash courts. All the old Clarendon schools which play rackets, as well as Malvern, have two courts, the rest have one. The last court to be built was at Harrow in 1965. At Cheltenham one of the two courts, which had been used for other purposes since 1939, was reopened in 1989.

Golf

Like lawn tennis, golf was a game that only came into its own at public schools in the 20th century. But in 1871 the following article appeared in *The Field*.

Inauguration of Golf at Radley College

Saturday, October 7 – As golfers were returning from the Northern Autumn Meetings to compete for the Westward Ho and Blackheath fixtures, a stray golfer was invited to Radley College, to be present at the inauguration of golf.

In the beautiful park belonging to Radley College, consisting of above 100 acres, the Warden has kindly consented to the Collegians laying out a golf course, which had been prepared temporarily to the best of their ability for the 8th. No sooner were the clubs and balls at hand than the muscular young fellows were swinging in all directions, above and to hand – topping, hacking, and every other mischance except driving the globe, and convincing themselves that the apparently easy feat of properly rising the small ball is not a simple effect of eye and strength.

The morning was spent in a quiet inspection, and trial with one of the masters and two youths who had some acquaintance with the game. The inaugural match, being fixed for the afternoon, was commenced as soon as the good things of the mid-day repast were despatched, in the grand old halls of Radley. Would anyone be surprised, when so much has been written lately in *The Field* and other journals and periodicals of the enthusiasm of golfers and the engross-

ing nature of the game of golf, that the Rev. the Warden should be an
approver of and a participator in the game, on its advent at the college
over which he presides? The foursome was well contested throughout,
the Warden contributing more than his share to the success, and
showing what a good cricket education and a correct eye will do in golf.
After the inaugural match was finished, the course was fixed for the
present, with certain improvements which will admit of extension. The
entire distance of nine holes is about 3330 yards, round the inner park,
which is eaten off by sheep, and consists of The Ricks, the Path, the
May, the Wood, the Elm Clump, the Firs, the Ridge, the Warden's and
the Home Holes; the places named being conspicuous objects, the fine
trees and clumps forming openings and obstacles, and the undulations
a pleasing variety. The clock tower of the Fives Court rising above the
roof of the Gymnasium, gives the leading mark to the Warden's Hole.
The last hole, sheltered in the trees which form the boundary of Radley
lawns and shrubberies, is indeed a home hole. Few of thousands who
on the Great Western Railway pass the bottom of the park are aware
of this charming spot,for the purpose of education and the propagation
of golf.

The Oldest Course in England?

When James VI became James I a golfing court came with him, and so
began golf in England at Blackheath.[4]

Royal Blackheath according to tradition was founded in 1608, at the
time the Scottish King was elected to the throne of England, and on
Blackheath Common he played his favourite game with his nobles. It
is doubtful if clubs or societies existed prior to the reign of Charles II,
much less golf clubs, and modern researchers among golf records set
the correct date of Royal Blackheath about 1787. Ed. W.E. Hughes
(1897), *Chronicles of Blackheath Golfers*

'According to the *Golfers Handbook* for 1953 the oldest golf club for
which they have evidence is the Honourable Company of Edinburgh
Golfers (under its then title Gentleman Golfers) in 1744. The earliest
written evidence of the existence of the Royal & Ancient is 1754. The
Handbook then gives a list of 36 Clubs between 1761 and 1869 and
all of them are Scottish except for 2 English and the Royal Bombay
in 1842. The 2 English ones are Old Manchester in 1818 and
Alnmouth in 1869. Two more clubs were founded in the 1860s,
Westward Ho! (Royal North Devon G.C.), and in 1869 Hoylake (Royal
Liverpool). The next oldest is West Lancashire started in 1872 or
1873.'[5] In the 1870s, with the introduction of the cheaper gutta-per-
cha ball, golf became more popular and more clubs were formed.
   So is Radley, in 1871, the sixth oldest course in England? Or were
there other private courses which are older? The course was ploughed
up for crops during the First World War; it was re-started in 1930.
After suffering a similar fate in the Second World War, it remained
out of use until 1985, when a professionally designed 9-hole course
was opened; and a club, affiliated to the English Golf Union, was
formed in 1992.

Chapter 8

The Twentieth Century

In the first half of the 20th century the social order remained broadly unchanged and unchallenged. The amateur ethos in sport was at its strongest. The distinction between those who played purely for enjoyment and those for whom it was a livelihood could hardly have been more clear, and the latter were regarded as socially inferior.

Cricket amateurs had private means, or a job which allowed them plenty of time to play. Some of the latter were public school masters, good enough cricketers to spend the summer holidays playing for a county. The Gentlemen v. Players match, though an attractive fixture, emphasised the divide. Other obvious distinctions were the official usage on scorecards and in the press of Mr D.R. Jardine and Hobbs, J.B., and the contrasted entrances to the field at Lord's, for instance, where amateurs (sometimes the captain alone) descended the Pavilion steps and professionals passed through a side gate.

In 1914 when Clifton and Tonbridge first played at Lord's, the M.C.C. were able to reinstitute a Lord's Public Schools Week, three two-day matches, Clifton and Tonbridge, Rugby and Marlborough, Cheltenham and Haileybury. Eton played Harrow a fortnight earlier. In 1861 *Bell's Life* had recorded '7000 persons on the ground on the First Day of Eton v. Harrow and 700 carriages of the nobility and gentry of England, filled with the rank, the fashion and the beauty of the country'. In 1914, on the eve of War, Wisden's estimated attendance of 38,000 over the two days bore witness to the enduring popularity of this oldest of continuous fixtures. The other Lord's Schools could not rival this, but two sets of schoolboys and their families and Old Boys amounted to a fair gate, swollen after Tea, as were the Tavern takings, by a vocal crowd of partisans from City offices. Being known as a Lord's School enhanced its reputation, and for those who played there it was the thrill of a lifetime. No other arena has so long a history or so powerful an aura within its sport worldwide.

The best public school cricketers had a high profile when they went up to Oxford or Cambridge, where they formed the bulk of the Eleven. The Universities were strong sides, often capable of defeating a county. A 'blue', particularly a cricket, rugger or rowing blue, was a cachet which could lead to a good job at home or in the Empire, where the Anglo-Egyptian Sudan was known as 'a country of Blacks ruled by Blues'. Like Eton v. Harrow, the Oxford and Cambridge cricket match, though less of a social occasion, was one of the great sporting events in the capital. This was true also for the Boat Race and the Varsity Rugger Match at Twickenham. All three events relied strongly on public school representation. The Boat Race attracted nationwide interest. Its unique character appealed even to those who knew nothing of rowing. In parts of London there was hardly a small boy who did not wear a light or dark blue favour for days before the race.

At Henley the Ladies' Plate attracted an increased number of college or school eights, which was one reason that Eton and Radley did not meet between the wars. This was a thinner period for Eton, compared with their past successes. They won in 1921, but did not reach another final. In 1925 Radley were in the final for the fifth time since 1861, which they lost to Lady Margaret B.C., Cambridge, by 2 lengths. In 1938 the *Daily Telegraph* headlines said it all: 'Radley win at Henley after Seventy-Seven Attempts – Two seconds Faster than Victorious London crew in Grand.' The time of 6 minutes 56 seconds equalled Eton's in 1911. But celebration would have been even greater had Eton beaten Pembroke, Cambridge in their semi-final, and given Radley the chance of what would surely have been victory at last over Eton in the Ladies' Plate. That victory came at Henley in 1945, but not in the Ladies' and not at Henley Royal Regatta. It was in the Hedsor Cup for schools in the one-day Royal Henley Regatta, so-called, after the end of war in Europe, but before the surrender of Japan. In the final Radley beat Eton and Bedford. Between the two World Wars Shrewsbury (who first entered in 1912) won the Ladies' twice, in 1924 and 1932, Eton once in 1921, and Radley once in 1938.

Because it was amateur and middle-class Rugby Union had a much stronger image at Oxford and Cambridge than Association Football, the national game. The centre of interest in soccer was the professional Football League and the F.A. Cup; but the amateur game was also very strong. The Amateur Football Association was founded in 1907 to take responsibility for the great number of clubs with unpaid players. By 1960 there were 'almost a hundred times more amateurs than professionals playing organised soccer in England'.[1] Their many strong leagues around London, the Athenian, Isthmian, Spartan, Corinthian and Nemean, show a distinct 'classical' influence in their foundation. The most famous amateur club, one not in a league, was the Corinthians. Founded in 1882 for 'Public School and University men', their Rule 7 was: 'The Club shall not compete for any challenge cup or any prizes of any description whatever.' They had been formed 'to raise the prestige and standards of English international football against Scotland'[2] who had been regularly winning. In this they succeeded. (This was before professional football was recognised in 1885.) 'They had the greatest influence in the game's formative years during the last decade of the 19th century.' In 1891 the penalty kick had been added to the Laws of the game. In a match in South Africa in 1903, 'they were determined to show that the game could be played in such a spirit that the referee would never be required to interfere on the ground of foul play'. When the referee awarded a penalty against the Corinthians, 'the captain ordered his goalkeeper to stand clear of the goal and offer no opposition to the point being scored. Not long afterwards the converse case occurred ... The Corinthians captain, taking the kick himself made no attempt to score a goal, but sent the ball over the touchline'.[3]

Today, this example of sportsmanship appears distinctly 'over the top'. Sportsmanship was a new concept, a product of the 19th century Christian gentleman ideal of Dr Arnold, a throwback perhaps to medieval chivalry, as exemplified in the 18th century by the French officer at Fontenoy with his request *'Que messieurs les Anglais tirent les premiers.'*

In sporting terms it was the 'muscular Christianity' which inspired Newbolt's line at Clifton 'Play up! play up! and play the game' and, in the United States, Grantland Rice's lines in 'Alumnus Football': 'For when the One Great Scorer comes to write against your name, He marks – not that you won or lost – But how you played the game!' 'It's not cricket' became a universal term for 'It's not fair or decent.' Sportsmanship puts team before the individual, and team spirit is paramount. Thomas Hughes has old Brooke say: 'I know I'd sooner win two School-house matches running than get the Balliol Scholarship any day.'

The Amateur ethos prevailed into the mid-20th century in most games, until Tennis, Athletics, Cricket and most recently Rugby Union all became professional at the top of their sport, as did much of Amateur Soccer. The century or more of amateur-led sport had propagated and preserved the ideal of Sportsmanship and exported it along with the games. This is not to say that professional sportsmen are any less sporting than are amateurs; but 'It matters not who won or lost, but how you played the game' is not the most likely post-match comment of a Premier League manager, and treating triumph and disaster just the same must be doubly hard for someone whose livelihood depends on winning an Olympic medal. Sportsmanship or 'Fairplay' is still regarded abroad as an English or British characteristic, and England's Fair Play Award at the soccer World Cup in Italy in 1990, and again at the European Cup in England in 1996 were valued consolation for losing on penalties to Germany in the semi-finals in both cases.

The second half of the 20th century has been in sharp contrast with its predecessor in the scale of the changes that have taken place in sport. After long years of exhausting war and post-war rationing and conscription, the 1960s saw a reaction to austerity, authority and military short-back-and-sides, particularly among the young, who had money to spend as never before. The new youth-led culture, visible in hair and clothes and everywhere audible in pop music, was readily embraced by public schoolboys who pre-war had themselves set the tone for youth, aided by the *Magnet*, featuring Harry Wharton and Billy Bunter's 'Greyfriars', with a readership among all classes. This social levelling down was reflected in the national games.

In 1963, in accordance with the spirit of the times, the distinction between amateur and professional was abolished in English first-class cricket. This brought to an end the annual Gents v. Players match, first contested in 1806. Also in 1963, the Gillette Cup the first one-day knock-out competition, was inaugurated, causing a re-scheduling of fixtures at Lord's. These developments eventually finished off Public Schools Week. The last matches were played in 1968, with the oldest fixture, Rugby v. Marlborough begun in 1871, continuing as a one-day game until 1972. Also ended was the series of one-day matches (1926-1968) between the Catholic schools Oratory and Beaumont, and when the latter ceased to exist, briefly Downside. Eton and Harrow remain at Lord's, now for one day only, and with considerably less of the garden party atmosphere. By 1997 the record was 52 wins for Eton, 44 for Harrow and 65 draws.

At Oxford and Cambridge, which embody amateur sporting tradition, the public schools have suffered further loss. The universities' new aim has been to attract many more maintained school pupils, and a new generation of dons did not think that sporting success for their college or university should be bought at the expense of a lowering of academic standards of entrance. This attitude affected all sports, but cricket especially because of the long hours spent away from books. The result has been that many of the best public school cricketers now go up to Durham or elsewhere, and Oxford and Cambridge cricket struggles to maintain a standard that justifies its first class status. The Lord's match now attracts few spectators. Rugby Union is in a stronger position not having had to rely quite so much on public school Old Boys, but it can seldom now compete on equal terms with the stronger clubs, as in the past. The introduction of professionalism into the game will further reduce competitiveness. On the river the keen rivalry between Oxford and Cambridge, the prestige earned by gaining a rowing blue, and the worldwide exposure of the Boat Race have attracted post-graduate oarsmen, especially from overseas, older men who are stronger and more experienced than the public school undergraduates they have replaced.

Rowing at schools has prospered nevertheless. More schools enter more crews at regattas and heads (of the river), culminating in the National Schools' Regatta at Nottingham, the biggest regatta in Britain in the number of crews entering. The more glamorous Henley follows this. Since the war only Eton have won the Ladies' Plate, in 1948, and for the 24th time in 1960; but Emanuel came close, losing in the 1967 Final to First and Third Trinity, Cambridge. In 1946 a new event exclusively for schools was inaugurated, the Princess Elizabeth Cup. Over fifty years it has been won by ten English schools, Eton, St Edward's, Hampton, Radley, St Paul's, Pangbourne,

Emanuel (all on the Thames), Bedford, Shrewsbury and Winchester; and by ten overseas schools (admitted from 1964), seven from the U.S.A., two from Canada (Ridley College five times in the '70s), and one from Australia.

Public school sportsmen have lost much of their influence at university and beyond, but within the schools themselves rowing is not the only sport which is in a healthy condition. Many more boys (and now girls too) play many more sports. Block match fixtures, made possible by improved transport facilities, are played simultaneously home and away, involving hundreds of boys, who pre-war would probably have had to watch the First Team match. With the building of Sports Halls and all-weather outdoor surfaces boys have been introduced to a far wider choice of sports to follow. More masters, accordingly, become involved to organise, coach and referee. In the 16th century Richard Mulcaster, ahead of his time, argued that one teacher should be responsible for both the physical and the intellectual welfare of a pupil. Many a master has found that involvement on the games field has eased his task in the classroom. Many schools encourage use of their new sporting facilities. This helps with the running costs, and also brings the school more into the local community to mutual benefit.

A sport which is making a comeback nationally, albeit still a modest one, is the royal and ancient game of Tennis. After a falling away in the 18th century Tennis was revived in England in the 19th. Between 1850 and 1922 30 courts were built. Today the game is strongest in England with 16 courts in use; in Scotland 2, France 2, Australia 5 and U.S.A. 7, a total of 32. In Britain the game is now known as Real Tennis, in Australia as Royal Tennis, and in the United States as Court Tennis; its late 19th century offspring, Lawn Tennis (a form of Longue Paume) having purloined its name. As in the 16th century two schools possess a Tennis Court, no longer Winchester and Eton, but Canford, which inherited one when the school was founded in a country house in 1923, and Oratory, where a court was built in 1989. Radley uses the Oxford court in Merton Street, and the three schools have a mini-National Schools Competition annually. Stowe, Haileybury and Hampton also play occasional matches. The Bristol & Bath Tennis Club is building a court on the playing field at Clifton College. The use of school courts by local clubs, as with Rackets courts, is a vital ingredient for the spread of the game's popularity in the future.

One sport abandoned at schools in the 1960s was boxing. The Marquess of Queensberry had produced his Rules in 1869, and the Amateur Boxing Association was founded, with amended rules, in 1880. This was about the time that many schools funded a Missioner for Church Missions in slum parishes of the capital and other cities. Their Boys' Clubs joined the London Federation of Boys' Clubs, where boxing was the most popular athletic activity. Many boys in the Clubs, as well as in the public schools were taught 'the Noble Art of Self-Defence' and learned self-confidence and self-control and a ready respect for their opponents. Some clubs like the Repton and Eton Clubs produced many fine boxers. When teenagers became bigger and stronger in the post-war years, the practice of boxing was considered damaging and potentially dangerous and was stopped at public schools.

It is sad that sport in the Maintained Sector has been reduced. Playing fields have been recklessly sold, many teachers are now less prepared to help in their leisure time, and in some schools competitive games have been abandoned as being unfair on the losers. On the continent local sporting clubs are mostly responsible for encouraging schoolchildren to take part in their sports and for helping to develop their fitness and skills. This is beginning to happen more in Britain. With so much money coming into the clubs from sponsorship and from television this is likely to benefit at least a minority of children.

A more egalitarian society, the international nature and government of most sports, professionalism and television billions to pay for it, have changed the face of sport. Today it is no longer the upper classes who decide the future of many sports, but the television companies which have bought a measure of control over them, and the television audience, including the couch potato and his overweight son, whose aptly named 'remote control' sets the viewing ratings and threatens to make the viewer the ultimate arbiter of our sporting future.

Notes

Chapter 1. Early Games

1. Benedetto Varchi (1503-63), *Storia fiorentina* 1527-38 (Augsburg, 1721).

2. Michelangelo Tenagli, *Libro di ricordi* quoted in Alfredo Lensi, *Il gioco del Calcio fiorentino* (Firenze, 1931).

3. Giovanni de' Bardi, *Discorso sopra il giuoco del Calcio fiorentino* (Firenze, 1673).

4. Alexander Sorel 'Le Jeu de la choule' in *Bulletin historique et philologique des travaux historiques et scientifiques* (Paris, 1894).

5. Anatole de Barthélemy, *Revue de Bretagne et de Vendée* (1859).

6. *Annales de Bretagne Vol. XXVII* Rennes University (Rennes 1912).

7. The Founding Statutes of Winchester College, first published in 1400, prohibited 'throwing of stones and balls or other things in chapel, cloister, stalls and hall, and also jumping, wrestling and other reckless and disorderly games in them' by which 'the walls, stalls, pictures and glass windows of sumptuous work may be defaced.' It was in fact an ancient custom in the secular church for the canons and other ministers of the church to play games, dance, leap and wrestle in churches. A.F. Leach, *History of Winchester College* (Duckworth, 1899).

8. Op. cit. Rennes University (1912).

9. One cannot help wondering if 'hurling' comes originally from *heuul* or *houl*, the Cornish for sun, similar to the Armorican *heol*, *héault*.

10. A. Ivan Rabey *Hurling at St Columb* (A.I. Rabey, 1969).

11. J.J. Jusserand *Sports et jeux d'exercice dans l'ancienne France* (Paris, 1901).

12. F.P. Magoun, Jnr., Professor of Comparative Literature at Harvard University. 'History of Football to 1871' in *Kölner Anglistiche Arbeiten Vol. 31* (Bochum-Langendreer, 1939).

13. William Windham (1750-1810), educated at Eton. M.P. for Norwich and elsewhere. Secretary for War under Pitt (1794-1801) and Lord Grenville (1806-7). He 'had a passion for the sports of the people – bull-baiting, cock-fighting and so forth – and he vigorously defended these diversions in Parliament against all attempts to suppress them.' 'Camping – a forgotten Norfolk game' by R.W. Ketton-Cremer in *Norfolk Archaeology* (Norfolk and Norwich Archaeological Society Vol. XXIV 1932).

14. Rev. W.T. Spurden *Supplementary Volume to Forby* (London 1858).

Chapter 2. The Public Schools

1. Steve Bailey 'Permission to Play: Education for Recreation and Distinction at Winchester College 1382-1680' in *The International Journal of the History of Sport, Vol.12 No. 1.* (Frank Cass, 1995).

2. op. cit. J.J. Jusserand (1901).

3. ibid.

4. ibid.

5. Julian Marshall, *The Annals of Tennis* (London, 1878).

6. ibid.

7. There was a melancholy aspect of the Royal Game. King Philip I was dead the same year, 1506, one of three monarchs who died from a chill after a game. The others were Henry I of Castile in 1217 and Louis X of France in 1316. In 1498 Charles VIII of France, going with his queen to watch a tennis match in the castle moat at Amboise, hit his head on the lintel of a low door, and subsequently died from the blow. In 1437 James I of Scotland, lodged for Christmas in the monastery of the Dominicans in Perth, trying to escape assassination at midnight, 'might have effected his escape into the deserted court-yard, and thence into the town, by a small passage through the stone wall; but this he had caused to be closed up three days previous, because in playing at his favourite game in the tennis-court without, the balls had been lost in the aperture.' Thomas Thomson (1894), *History of the Scottish People* Blackie & Son.

8. *Enciclopedia Italiana di scienze lettere ed arti* (Istituto Giovanni Treccani, 1935).

9. H. Staunton, *The Great Schools of England* (Sampson, Low, Son & Marston, 1903).

10. Rev. H.W. Phillott in *A Charterhouse Miscellany* by R.L. Arrowsmith (London, 1982).

11. H.J.C. Blake, *Reminiscences of Eton* (Chichester, 1831).

12. W. Veale, *From a New Angle* (P. & G. Wells Ltd., 1957).

13. G.S. Davies, *Charterhouse in London* (John Murray, 1921).

14. op. cit. Rev. H.W. Phillott (1982).

15. Frederick Lillywhite, *Cricket Scores 1746-1826* (Frederick Lillywhite, 1862).

16. Thomas Balston, *Dr Balston at Eton* (Macmillan, 1952).

17. E.W. Howson & G. Townsend Warner, *Harrow School* (Edward Arnold, 1898).

18. At Rugby the whole school of 300 or so took part. The juniors acted as goal-keepers, guarding the line against a touch-down which earned a 'try' at goal, but no points. At Harrow, when a base (goal) was scored, ends were changed and 'the small guardians of the base who had failed to protect it were sent flying to the other base by a series of kicks administered by the players of their own side all down the ground.' (op. cit. E.W. Howson & G. Townsend Warner 1898). At Winchester, coatless and shivering, they guarded the touchline behind a rope. 'On Fridays when there was a chapel service from eleven to twelve, the word used to be passed round amongst the fags in all seriousness, with some faint recollection perhaps of the Tishbite on Mount Carmel, to "pray for rain"' W. Tuckwell, *The Ancient Ways: Winchester 50 years Ago* (Macmillan, 1893). In 1840 pity was taken on them, and a canvas screen replaced the human walls; but spectators could not see and canvas caught the wind, so from 1866 netting was used instead. Today the ropes and netting are an integral part of Winchester Football, and a 'canvas' is the name for a football pitch.

19. For the Old Rugbeian match of 1871 'fifty-seven caps followed up for the School while the old boys played about ten more' – 124 forwards. Very large numbers played in the two other 'great' matches, The Sixth v. The School and the Two Cock Houses v. The Rest. Other Big Side games were about 30-a-side, and House Matches were 20-a-side.

20. *Illustrated Sporting News* (London, 31 March 1866).

21. The Public Schools Act of 1868 and the Endowed Schools Act of 1869 dealt with existing secondary education for the upper and middle classes.

The Education Act of 1870 was the first step in providing universal, compulsory and free education for 5 to 13 year olds. There was no provision in the Act for playing games or for any form of physical education. It was not until 1900 that the Board of Education advised H.M. Inspectors that games were a suitable alternative to the Swedish drill or physical exercises introduced by local school boards. The 1902 Education Act led to the provision of games-playing facilities for both elementary and new secondary schools.

22. Marlborough, Sedbergh, Harrow, Clifton, Fettes, Haileybury.

23. It is curious to mark from the score sheets of the forties the change from under to round-arm bowling by the immense increase in wides. Hitherto these had naturally been an almost negligible item. Henceforth, for a period, they are nearly always double figures, and constantly between 20 and 30. Edward Rutter, *Cricket Memories* (William & Norgate, 1925). He was at Rugby 1853-62.

24. Rev. T.D. Raikes, *Fifty Years of St Peter's College, Radley* (James Parker, 1897).

25. H.E.M. Icely, *Bromsgrove School through Four Centuries* (Blackwell, 1953).

Chapter 3. Fives

1. William Rogers, *Reminiscences* (Kegan Paul, Trench & Co., 1888).

Chapter 4. Cricket

1. Harrow was the first school to employ a professional coach in the 1820s.

2.   Eton boatmen,
        Harrow gentlemen,
        Westminster scoundrels,
        Winchester scholars. [19th-century Rhyme]

3. W.A. Fearon, *The Passing of Old Winchester* (Private Circulation, 1924).

Chapter 5. Football

1. R.G. Graham, 'The Early History of the Football Association' in *The Badminton Magazine of Sports and Pastimes* (London, 1899).

2. op. cit. H.J.C. Blake.

3. A game with some similarities to Football at Eton and Harrow, and indeed to most other versions of Football then being played – basically 'soccer' with 'rugger' offside. Before hacking was outlawed anyone alone with the ball in enemy territory was liable to be summarily and painfully hacked down.

4. F.A.D. Bland in *Durham School Register* 3rd. edition.

5. R.I.H. Gollop in the *Centenary of Joining the R.F.U. Programme* (King's School Canterbury, 1972).

6. Captain F. Markham *Recollections of a Town Boy at Westminster* (Edward Arnold, 1903).

7. R.S. Stanier, *Magdalen School* (Basil Blackwell, 1958).

8. A.G. Bradley, A.C. Champneys & J.N. Baines, *History of Marlborough College* (John Murray, 1923).

9. Sebastian Rivington, *History of Tonbridge School* (Rivingtons, 1898).

10. Bryan Matthews, *By God's Grace* (Whitehall Press, 1984).

11. P.H.M. Bryant, *Harrow* (Blackie & Son, 1936).

12. Frank Miles & Graeme Cranch, *King's College School: The First 150 Years* (King's College School, 1979).

13. op. cit. Rev. T.D. Raikes (1897).

14. Arthur Budd, C.B. Fry, T.A. Cook & B.F. Robinson, *Football* (Lawrence & Bullen, 1897).

15. G. Gruggen & J. Keating, *Stonyhurst* (Kegan Paul, Trench, Trübner & Co. Ltd., 1901).

16. A. Clutton-Brock, *Eton* (G. Bell & Sons, 1900).

17. Angelo Raine, *History of St Peter's School, York* (G. Bell & Sons Ltd., 1926).

18. Lees Knowles 'Rugby School: Games' in *Great Public Schools* (Edward Arnold).

19. H. Edwards 'Football in the 1870s.' *The Christ's Hospital Book* (Hamish Hamilton, 1953).

20. Ian Bailey at Manchester Grammar School.

21. Old Wykehamists, *Winchester College* 1393-1893 (Edward Arnold, 1893).

22. R.B. Mansfield, *School-life at Winchester College* (D. Nutt, 1893).

23. *Merchiston Castle School Register* (H. & J. Pillans & Wilson, 1906).

24. J.D. Carleton, *Westminster School* (Rupert Hart-Davies, 1965).

25. op. cit. R.G. Graham (1899).

26. Barnes 'recruited from the rowing element and the noted army cramming establishments of Messrs. Baty and Inchbald'; Crystal Palace (not the present club); Kensington Proprietary Grammar School, Kensington Square, from 1831 until 1896 when High Street, Kensington underground station was built there; Royal Engineers used 'military football tactics' to introduce the 'combination' style of play, and won the F.A. Cup in 1875 (all officers); Sheffield F.C. founded in 1857 with a nucleus of Old Boys of Sheffield Collegiate School (1836, now King Edward VII School), is the oldest surviving football club in the world (outside academe). It was permitted to play to its own rules, different from London's, but like them they 'embodied the best points' from the various Public Schools' rules, copies of which had been sent to them on request; Wanderers, founded by Old Harrovians, became a powerful Public Schools Old Boys Club, winning the F.A. Cup five times in the first seven years; Worlabye House (Baty's) was a cramming establishment for army entry to Woolwich and Sandhurst.

27. F.A. Cup 1877-8. 1st round lost 0-1 to 1st Surrey Rifles. 1878-9. 1st round beat Rochester 4-2. 2nd round lost 0-1 to Clapham Rovers who lost in the final to Old Etonians.

28. op. cit. R.G. Graham (1899).

29. Fred Walters *Sheffield Football Club Centenary History* (Sheffield Football Club 1957).

Chapter 6. Boating

1. Lawrence Tanner, *Westminster School* (Country Life Ltd., 1934).

2. W.B. Woodgate, *Boating* (Longmans Green, 1891).

3. A.D. Coleridge, *Eton in the Forties* (Richard Bentley & Son, 1898).

4. op. cit. William Rogers (1888).

5. R.H. Blake-Humfrey, *Eton Boating Book* (F.P. Williams & Son, 1869).

6. op. cit. William Rogers (1888).

7. Sir H.C. Maxwell Lyte, *History of Eton College* (Macmillan, 1911).

8. op. cit. R.H. Blake-Humfrey (1869).

9. Rev. C.A. Wilkinson, *Reminiscences of Eton in Keyte's Time* (Hunt & Blackett, 1888).

10. op. cit. William Rogers (1888).

11. An Old Colleger, *Eton of Old or 80 Years Since* (Griffith Farrn & Co. Ltd., 1882).

12. op. cit. Sir H.C. Maxwell Lyte (1911).

13. ibid.

14. ibid.

15. W.K.R. Bedford, *Rowing at Westminster* (Kegan Paul, Trench, Trübner & Co., 1890).

16. F.H. Forshall, *Westminster School Past and Present* (Wyman & Sons, 1884).

17. *Bell's Life in London and Sporting Chronicle*.

18. op. cit. F.H. Forshall (1884).

19. *Bell's Life in London and Sporting Chronicle*.

20. A randan is a boat in which the middle of the three rowers pulls a pair of sculls, stroke and bow an oar each.

21. op. cit. F.H. Forshall (1884).

22. op. cit. W.B. Woodgate (1891).

23. A.C. Ainger, *Memories of Eton 60 Years Ago* (John Murray, 1917).

24. *Westminster School Water Ledger* (1884).

25. op. cit. Lawrence Tanner (1934).

26. *The Field*.

27. *Oxford Chronicle*.

28. *The Era*.

29. op. cit. A.C. Ainger (1917).

30. *Oxford University Herald*.

31. op. cit W.B. Woodgate (1891).

32. The title is a mystery for when the trophy appeared in 1846 it turned out to be not a Plate but a handsome ewer. It has been suggested that it was given by the 'Ladies' of Henley, but there is no record of this. Richard Burnell (1989), *Henley Royal Regatta* William Heinemann in association with Gieves & Hawkes.

33. op. cit. A.D. Coleridge (1898).

34. op. cit. A.C. Ainger (1917).

35. William Oliver, *Rough Notes and Reminiscences*.

36. H.T. Steward, *Henley Royal Regatta* (Grant Richards, London, 1903).

Chapter 7. Late 19th-century Games

1. John Timbs, *School Days of Eminent Men* (Kent & Co., London, 1862).

2. John Armitage, *Rackets, Squash Rackets, Tennis, Fives, Badminton* (Seeley Service & Co., 1933).

3. ibid.

4. Horace Hutchinson, *The History of the Game of Golf* (Longmans Green, 1902).

5. R.H. Goodwin.

Chapter 8. The 20th century

1. A.H. Fabian and G. Green, *Association Football Vol. 3* (Caxton Publishing Co. Ltd., 1960).

2. ibid.

3. ibid.

Index